BECOMING A
SUPERHERO

BECOMING A SUPERHERO

AWAKEN YOUR SUPERPOWERS AND
INSPIRE THE MAGIC IN OTHERS

MARINA DESTINEE PAUL

NEW DEGREE PRESS

BECOMING A SUPERHERO

Awaken Your Superpowers and Inspire the Magic in Others

ISBN   978-1-63676-856-4   *Paperback*

          978-1-63730-186-9   *Kindle Ebook*

          978-1-63730-300-9   *Ebook*

CONTENTS

*To my mom, who taught me the greatest thing you
can do is create music, dance when you hear it, and
pull people onto the dance floor with you.
Your effervescent energy and unconditional love for life in
the face of tremendous adversity is why I know I can find
the disco sparkle in the darkness and be good to others, no
matter what. I carry your dance deep in my soul.
I'll see you on the other side of the ping pong table.
I love you, my Superhero.*

Marines

PART 1

SUPERHEROES TAKE FLIGHT

CHAPTER 1

CALLING ALL FUTURE SUPERHEROES

────────

BREATHING

Breathing is the first thing we experience when we enter this world and the last thing we do when we leave it. In many ways, it is the gateway to our being; it gives us the power to live. Breathing connects our subconscious to our conscious— the acts we do without noticing and the acts we choose to do willingly. We breathe shorter and faster when we feel anxious, deeper when we calm ourselves, and smoother when we are leveled.

To breathe means to be alive. To not breathe means to suffocate. Suffocation is the COVID-19 pandemic, a disease that started at the end of 2019 and attacked peoples' lungs, killing millions; suffocation is the knee on Black peoples' necks literally and figuratively, as racism permeates the foundation of America; suffocation is the California wildfires whose flames ravage communities and whose ashes sizzle the bronchi in peoples' lungs.

Suffocation is the suffering that created this book, but breathing ... breathing is the hope through which I wrote this book.

How do you breathe in the midst of suffering?

MOVIE SUPERHEROES VS. HUMAN SUPERHEROES

The movies tell us a Superhero will come to save us from our suffering. Their superpowers make them superhuman; they possess some force beyond scientific understanding or the laws of nature. As a kid, I thought only the legitimate Superheroes made it onto my LIFE Cinnamon Cereal box. I would hold my gaze on the back of my box as I robotically lifted soggy cinnamon wheat squares into my mouth. The world in which we grow up memorializes Superheroes by stamping them onto our cereal boxes, conditioning us as we get ready for our days.

Superheroes make us feel confident, powerful, and protected. They use their powers to help others at all costs, and they are willing to fail and fall down for the good of everyone else. They also show us that we can harness our own power. Ultimately, how a Superhero exercises their power for good is what separates them from being a villain. Their legacy is their humanity and how they touch the human heart, reminding us how much we need one another and our communities.

While humans may not have supernatural qualities, in order to breathe again we need Superhero strength in human form. Human Superheroes are far more heroic than those from comic books because they are 100 percent human, 100 percent of the time. They don't have a serum running through their veins helping them shoot out electricity when a villain invades their city, yet they still perform heroic acts that make it seem as though they possess some sort of magical ability. They use their humanity to put out fires, clean up the ashes, and make the air clean enough to breathe again.

While I'm still on my own quest for Superheroism, I'm here to tell you about real-life Superheroes who energize me—the people I've found who use their human superpowers to lead their communities out of suffocation.

INNER SUPERHERO

My journey toward discovering my superpowers began with my college soccer coach, Lyndse Hokanson. Lyndse taught me that in order to be great in this world and find fulfillment, we must uncover our unique abilities and use them as a force for good. She showed me how to rise out of darkness, find light, and bring others along with me.

When I graduated and left Lyndse along with the sports foundation I built myself for eighteen years, I thought I was ready for the world. I had been a three-year captain of the Georgetown Women's Soccer Team, our team was ranked in the top five in the country, and I received All-American accolades. I graduated from Georgetown University with two degrees, and I headed into a Director role at my first job. I mastered making everything on the outside appear perfect, but my deep-rooted mental health issues and insecurities overcame me when I could no longer hide them behind sports.

I didn't feel comfortable exposing my goofy, eccentric, and competitive athlete personality alongside my ADHD-diagnosed brain. Instead, I felt trapped trying to fit my 6'o" frame and head of bouncing, unorganized curls into a well-mannered, poised, and quiet shell of a girl who cared about simple things like gossiping. I tried to escape this world, while simultaneously convincing myself it was the way my life was *supposed to be.*

Slowly, I started removing the things that made me feel imprisoned and adding what made me feel free. As part of my healing process, I found myself yearning to become like the women I admired—those who had successfully built winning teams, were passionate, owned their individuality, and, no matter what, left each person better than they found them.

I embarked on a journey to find women who possessed these Superhero qualities while also digging deep to find the feelings of confidence and joy Lyndse had once helped me embody. I realized the importance of representation and how seeing someone with whom I resonated helped me believe in myself. I reimagined what I wanted my life to be like and how my own superpowers could help me conquer my world.

In the process of meeting incredible women I aspired to emulate, I also engaged in a new Millennial wave of the Women's Movement. This movement, known as the Girlboss era, seemed to champion female empowerment and embody "unapologetic ambition."[1] Women supporting

---

1   Leigh Stein, "The End of the Girlboss is Here," Gen Medium, June 22, 2020.

women? I was in! However, I soon realized the movement talked about Sisterhood and female empowerment as a trend and a hot topic rather than actually taking it seriously. I noticed some women were quick to praise other women in their fight against the patriarchy but were also often the first to talk negatively behind their backs. The movement's foundation felt rooted in fighting more for individual power rather than collective power for the diverse interests and nature of women. I studied and explored how we could reimagine a women's movement built on teamwork and Sisterhood between all women, and could, in turn, help *all* women rise.

By studying a breadth of women and the relationships between them while introspectively assessing my own life experiences, I discovered the key components that define Superheroism aren't limited to a certain industry or field, and they especially aren't limited to a skin color. It's also important to note that Superheroism isn't limited to gender, but in this book, it is.

What separates Superheroes from everyone else is what they do for others in the process of excelling in their life's work. Superheroism is a lifelong journey and response to adversity, while still taking into account the greater good. In order to start this journey, I learned we need to confront our inner monsters, find our worth, build a diverse Sisterhood, then repeat the process throughout our lives.

The women outlined in this book don't look the same. They don't come from the same towns or states. They don't have the same skin color. The way they speak is different.

Their sexuality is different. Their experiences are different. They have built careers in professional sports, venture capital, law, technology, and the United States Armed Forces. Their titles include Olympic Gold Medalist, Hall of Fame Coach, Principal Investor, General Counsel, CEO, and Lieutenant Colonel. What these Superheroes do have in common are certain qualities that we can all aspire to in our own lives.

This book is for women who have an earnest desire to become leaders and who are looking for examples of female mentorship and leadership. Some of you may be hitting all of your goals and killing it in your career and personal life. If that's you, then this book will help challenge you to recognize the type of impact you want to have, not only for a company's bottom line (or *your* company's), but for the sake of the human lives with whom you interact.

If you're like me, maybe your latest transition knocked you off your path and you're trying to find what you're truly passionate about. This book will help you forge your own trail when things don't go as planned by rebuilding your confidence and validating your worth. Maybe you don't fall into either of these categories, but you are here, making an effort. Never dismiss the courage it takes to start.

By the end of this book, you—*yes, you*—will know how you can harness your powers beyond anything you thought you were capable of to *become a Superhero*.

If I could create my own cereal box, I would swap the comic book Superheroes with the faces of the women I interviewed. I would feature their stories—the mountains they climbed over and over again as they trailblazed paths and installed ladders to help bring up other women with them.

Each of us has tremendous talents and life to breathe into a world of suffering. Our unique DNA helps create our superpowers and abilities to have a Superhero effect on the lives we touch. We just need to embark on our lifelong mission to find our superpowers.

For everyone who reads this book, I hope you feel the same joy and inspiration I did when I had the pleasure of interviewing these Superheroes and find comfort in my journey of finding my inner Superhero. I hope this book compels you to go after your wildest ambitions and to not make excuses for anybody. Lastly, I hope these women's stories show you how much you matter to this world and how profound of an impact your unique abilities can have on every life you touch.

Get ready to unleash your superpowers.

CHAPTER 2

DEFINING A SUPERHERO

THE SUPERHERO EFFECT

While I'd love to claim credit, the original idea of human Superheroism came from one of the most successful collegiate coaches in the history of college sports, Valorie Kondos Field, or "Miss Val," as her athletes call her. Miss Val was never a gymnast, and before being hired as a choreographer by a local gym, she had never even held a job in gymnastics. Yet, during her twenty-nine-year tenure as UCLA's gymnastics head coach, Miss Val won seven NCAA Championships, twenty-two Regional Championships, and eighteen Pac-12 Championships. She coached forty-six US National team members and half of the members of the last two US Gymnastics Olympic teams. Miss Val earned the title of West Region Coach of the Year, was a four-time National Coach of the Year, and was one of only two active coaches to be inducted into the UCLA Athletic Hall of Fame. In 2019, the year Miss Val officially retired from collegiate coaching, she earned the title, Pac-12 Coach of the Century.[2]

---

2   "Valorie Kondos Field '97: 2019 Professional Achievement Award," UCLA: UCLA Alumni, April 1, 2019.

Her coaching style—later defined as Superheroism—is unparalleled, especially in the world of gymnastics where perfectionism persists at the cost of an athlete's mental and physical well-being. If you watch videos of Miss Val coaching, you will see her gently grabbing her athletes faces, looking them in the eyes, and speaking words of encouragement before their routine or when they are having an off day at practice. You'll see her dancing on the sidelines as her athletes perform their floor routines to a remix of The Jackson 5 and Beyoncé. She breathed charisma into a sport in which, from the outside, being serious and poised seemingly earns you a higher score. She showed the sport of gymnastics that not only can you be a champion, but you can also have the time of your life doing it.

Growing up, Miss Val's dream was to be a ballerina, in part because many ballet teachers told her that her physique didn't fit the look of a typical ballerina. They said her head was too large, her neck was too short, and her feet were too little. However, despite all the physical requirements she lacked, her teachers told her she was a talented dancer. Miss Val carried body shaming with her throughout her coaching; she wanted not just her athletes but also her coaches to feel comfortable with who they were and how they looked. Miss Val said, "Unique is so much more fun than status quo."[3]

Growing up, Miss Val wanted to try gymnastics, but her parents wouldn't allow her to add yet another discipline to

---

3   "How Miss Val Became a Gymnastics Coaching Legend," *Player's Tribune*, April 25, 2019, video, 10:52.

her full schedule of schoolwork, ballet, piano lessons, and Camp Fire Girls membership. The summer of her high school junior year, Miss Val was looking for a job and called a local gymnastics team to see if they needed a dance coach. While they didn't have the budget for a dance coach, they did have the budget for a pianist to play the floor exercise music. Miss Val took the job, which eventually launched her into becoming one of the premier dance coaches and choreographers in the world of artistic gymnastics.

After twenty-nine seasons as the UCLA Gymnastics head coach, Miss Val reflected, "If you would've told me I was going to be the UCLA Gymnastics head coach, to me that would have been like going to the moon with Mikhail Baryshnikov. That was not happening." She sat there, shaking her head and saying, "How did that happen?"[4]

Since she has coached some of the world's most elite athletes and won the most prestigious awards in collegiate athletics, I asked Miss Val what separates good athletes from Olympians. Miss Val responded, "A great athlete puts in the work, dots the I's and crosses the T's, and does their job or role well." An athlete shows up and gets a little better every day. Then, Miss Val's face brightened, as she expelled some wisdom and magic:

---

4   Ibid.

"The difference between a great athlete and a Superhero is that Superheroes do everything great athletes do, but Superheroes actually lift everyone up in the process. Superheroes achieve, oftentimes, almost unimaginable things of excellence by lifting other people up. When you reach outside of yourself and lift people up, you become a greater sum of all of your parts, and you become greater than you would have sticking in your own little bubble."

VALORIE KONDOS FIELD

Superheroism is a choice that exists within all of us. It's not a measure of whether or not we go to the Olympics; instead, it's a measure of what we do to elevate the lives of others. When we lift up others, we not only become better versions of ourselves, but our impact has a compounding effect. Like the transfer of magic, each person continues to uplift the lives they touch. This is called the *Superhero Effect*.

Superheroism is the only way to raise this world higher than we can imagine, even in the darkest of times.

COACH'S OFFICE
After Miss Val retired, she delivered a TED Talk, "Why Winning Doesn't Always Equal Success." In this talk, Miss Val described her relationship with one of her athletes, Kyla Ross, who Miss Val called "one of the greatest gymnasts in the

history of the sport" and "a Superhero."[5] Kyla is the only athlete to have ever achieved all three pinnacles of her sport at each level: she's a National Champion, a World Champion, and an Olympic Gold Medalist.

Miss Val recounts one particular day in 2018 when Kyla came into Miss Val's office and sat on her couch. Every college athlete knows about the proverbial head coach's couch. Depending on your relationship with your coach and your reason for being in that office, that couch can feel fluffy and comfortable—a place where you feel safe and welcomed. Other times, it can feel lumpy and put you on edge, especially during an awkward conversation that makes you leave feeling both uneasy and slightly defeated.

That day, Kyla made small talk about all of the things going on in her life and her future, but Miss Val could sense she was on her couch for a different reason. Miss Val gave Kyla time, knowing that what Kyla really had to say would eventually come out. Finally, it did. She told Miss Val that she had been sexually abused by the former USA Gymnastics team doctor.[6] Miss Val told me:

5   "Valorie Kondos Field: Why Winning Doesn't Always Equal Success," TEDWomen 2019, December 2019, video, 15:41.
6   Ibid.

"It was the first time that Kyla had shared [this] with anyone ... Larry Nassar, the former USA Gymnastics team doctor, was later convicted of being a serial child molester. Kyla came forward and joined the army of Nassar survivors who shared their stories and used their voices to invoke positive change for our world."

VALORIE KONDOS FIELD

Miss Val had always provided a safe space for her athletes to come and talk with her, and Kyla's visit that day amplified the importance of this space. Miss Val allowed Kyla to express herself and talk openly about one of—if not the most—traumatizing experiences of her life, an experience that was later exposed to the entire world. Many of Miss Val's coaching coworkers advised her not to bring up distractions that would take away from the gymnasts' focus. However, Miss Val knew the humanity of her athletes mattered so much more than their abilities to perform. Taking care of her athletes as human beings was forever her greatest priority as their coach.

That year, UCLA won the NCAA National Championship, making them the number one team in all of college gymnastics. After the win, Kyla walked up to Miss Val and said, "I literally felt myself walk taller as the season went on, and when I walked onto that championship floor, I felt invincible." Because of Miss Val's Superhero touch that created a safe place for Kyla to just be, Miss Val lifted the weight of trauma, abuse, and judgement off of her athlete's shoulders and brought out her magic.

Miss Val didn't only ask her athletes to be vulnerable and trusting with her, but she, too, reciprocated this vulnerability, particularly when she learned of her breast cancer diagnosis. After weighing the legal ramifications against the lesson of strength and resilience she wanted to teach her athletes, she asked them if they wanted to feel the malignant tumor in her breast one day at practice. One of her athletes, Sadiqua Bynum, reached out her hand to touch Miss Val's breast, then remarked how weird it felt touching her coach's breast. "No," Miss Val corrected her. "You're feeling what a malignant tumor feels like."[7] Miss Val saw this as a moment to teach her athletes to confront the realities in life we can't control—like cancer—and how to choose resilience at all costs.

Miss Val effectively uses gymnastics as an avenue to teach valuable life lessons, and she does so through exceptional leadership and mentorship of young student-athletes. "It's not about winning and losing, it's about choreographing your life and owning the choices you make."[8]

MAINTAINING SUPERHERO STATUS
Superhero status doesn't only apply to athletics. As Miss Val told me, Superheroism is a mindset followed by action, whether you're in the gym or in the grocery store.

---

7 Dvora Meyers, "Valorie Kondos-Field Let Her Gymnasts Feel Her Malignant Breast Tumor," *Deadspin*, September 22, 2017.

8 "About," Official Miss Val, accessed January 24, 2021.

"How do we individually want to model being a Superhero? What is our personal definition of daily success, and what does it look like?"

VALORIE KONDOS FIELD

When we look at top programs, whether that be in athletics or business, we see that money, resources, and top talent usually equal "success." The most highly regarded companies and environments, like top banking institutions and Olympic teams, measure success through transactional performance indicators such as highest revenue and most wins. Their high performance attracts top talent. As a society, we rarely equate success with joy and having fun. Yet, under Miss Val's leadership, UCLA Gymnastics had all three: championships, joy, and fun. Miss Val described her relationship with hundreds of her athletes as "remarkable" and "something she never takes for granted."[9] She also says that her athletes and her coaching staff continue to be her family. Top talent will eventually flee a transactional environment to achieve something greater than what they've experienced before: joy and the ability to express their individuality while still winning championships, much like UCLA Gymnastics.

Through her Superheroism, Miss Val has shown us that the definition of lasting success relies on a team-first mentality—bringing out the best in yourself and in others during both the highest of highs and lowest of lows. When this kind of

---

9   "How Miss Val Became a Gymnastics Coaching Legend," *Player's Tribune*, April 25, 2019, video, 10:52.

support, camaraderie, and motivation is achieved, every-day women can lift off the ground, take flight, and achieve the unimaginable.

CHAPTER 3

FIRST BUT NOT LAST

***

SANCTIFY BOOTY

I remember the first time I met Jasmine "Jaz" Graham. I had my first job out of college, working for a protein-bottled coffee start-up in New York City. Our marketing strategy was to penetrate the NYC boutique fitness scene and become the number one energy product that every gym owner, coach, and gym-goer put into their bodies. These gym-goers had tried all the latest trends in workout technology and performance, from gripped crew socks with breathable mesh to CBD-infused sleep pills that allow you to recover in six hours for a 5:00 a.m. workout. It was insane, but we wanted in.

We had our target list of gyms we wanted to supply—the ones where the top influencers go to hang out—followed by a list of five hundred other gyms in NYC. We tiered them out based on location and resonation with our brand.

One day, I received a call from my coworker who played college football and ran track at a competitive Pac-12 university. He also happened to look like an action figure.

He said, "Marina, I just got my a** kicked in this workout."

I laughed and said, "*You* did? No way! Which one?" I thought it had to have been one of the "Top 10 Workout Classes in NYC" printed in the latest issue of *Men's Fitness Magazine.*

He said, "The class is called 'Sanctify Booty.' This woman named Jaz Graham taught it at her studio, Fitness Sanctuary. I was the only guy in the class, and I died." I cracked up thinking about someone with the athleticism of a professional football player getting smoked in a booty class.

He put Jaz on the phone, and we had a brief conversation about getting our product into her gym. Jaz was one of the first Black women to own her own fitness studio in NYC, even though there were over two thousand gyms there. NYC is globally considered one of the most competitive markets for boutique fitness, largely because of the variety of classes offered and the amount of money people are willing to spend.[10] Jaz's goal was to create a destination for women with varying levels of physical fitness to learn how they could use exercise as a vehicle to gain confidence in themselves and power a healthy lifestyle.

Jaz and I developed a strong relationship over the next six months. Showing up for one of her classes would turn into multiple hour-long conversations at her studio. She was the kind of person to whom you wanted to tell all of your secrets

---

10 "Fitness Market Profile: New York City," After Pass, Partner Empowerment by Class Pass, accessed February 19, 2021.

and listen to her philosophies on life. I wanted to know what new meditation she was trying or what sermon she had been listening to.

Jaz's passion for helping others through fitness stemmed from her finding fitness as an outlet for herself. When Jaz first graduated college, she worked as a paralegal in preparation for law school. She soon learned that her true love was fashion, and she ended up working for prestigious brands such as Liz Claiborne and Calvin Klein before eventually becoming Vice President of Sales for two of Jay-Z's brands, Rocawear Big & Tall and Rocawear Loungewear. After she was laid off in 2008, her passion for running inspired her to start her fitness business.

That same year, she founded Pace For Success, a bootcamp-style workout focused on building strength for endurance runners. After the success of her bootcamps that required her to lug fitness equipment all around Brooklyn and Manhattan, she opened her first boutique gym named Fit Factory NYC in 2012. In 2017, she created Fitness Sanctuary, a home where she could rent out space to fitness professionals and teach her High Intensity Interval Training and personal training classes.

COMPOSITION NOTEBOOK
I will never forget the day I quit my job and walked out of the office building onto Wall Street. Despite being on one of the busiest streets in NYC, I felt completely alone. I didn't know who to call or what to do, but I needed to feel loved and comforted and know that everything was going to be okay.

So, I called Jaz.

"Jaz, I quit my job, I don't know where to go. Can I come see you?"

She said, "Come home."

I went straight to Fitness Sanctuary, and Jaz spent four hours comforting me and helping me create an action plan. Knowing how important my faith is to me, she said adamantly, "We're going to have weekly check-ins, and I want you to listen to this podcast from one of my favorite pastors on being resilient in faith and having faith in yourself." Jaz had made leaps of faith by herself, and I wholeheartedly trusted her guidance.

I asked her how she made the decision to jump not only into a new industry, but into self-employment. She said it all begins with sticking to your values and figuring out how you want to feel, what you want your days to look like, and what you want your tribe of people to be like. Jaz said, "Whatever I do, I want to feel like I'm making a difference in the world. I want to make people's lives better. Most importantly, I want to feel passion."

Jaz told me to buy a notebook immediately and fill it with my ideas and feelings. "Dump it all in there!" she exclaimed. My $1.80 Mead Composition Notebook from a CVS in Midtown Manhattan is now my most cherished possession. In it, I allowed myself to be vulnerable in ways I never have before. It holds my deepest insecurities and my grandest ideas. It's a notebook that many people possess, yet its contents are my brain and my guts—something no one but me possesses. This notebook is how Jaz helped me narrow in on my values and re-discover my imagination.

BUSINESS CARDS

In the fitness industry, there is a heightened expectation for one's physical appearance; your body becomes your business card. A particular physical aesthetic and a specific set of parameters for one's body type outweigh a high standard of performance. Biologically, however, this is not a realistic way of measurement; even if every human being ate exactly the same and worked out in the same ways, everyone's body would still look different. Yet, chasing an impossible idea of bodily perfection is how the industry thrives.

Jaz said her mom helped her love herself and understand what makes her unique, especially because she was an industry *first* in many situations.

> "There will always be somebody in the world that has better attributes than I do—prettier hair, a nicer nose, more money. But you know what? I'm Jaz, and what I bring to what I do, no one else can bring."
>
> JASMINE GRAHAM

It's not about fitting inside of the unrealistic parameters of perfection, but rather understanding what makes you *not* fit into those parameters and having confidence in your uniqueness.

In 2018, Jaz found out she has Hashimoto's Disease, an autoimmune disease in which her thyroid attacks itself. As a result, she gained a lot of weight in a short period of time. She woke up exhausted every morning and getting on the scale was painful. Jazz said, "My body was fighting me, and I felt like a stuffed sausage in spandex. I had to tell myself daily, 'I love you,' and come to terms with the fact that my state of being was temporary." Jaz was training people, teaching classes, working out, and fueling herself well, but the symptoms of weight gain, fatigue, brain fog, and exhaustion consumed her. She knew in order to achieve positive self-actualization, she needed to check in with her self-talk. She said, "If we're comparing ourselves to others, what's really going on with us? How are we feeling today? The stress we impart on ourselves to be like others reflects our internal wounds."

These moments of self-reflection remind me of my college soccer film sessions. Film sessions are designed to help you and your team understand how well you played and how you can improve from a previous game or practice. We not only watched films of ourselves, but also of our opponents in order to understand how to beat them. Film sessions usually occurred in a dark room with scattered desks. All the coaches sat in the front row with the exception of one who sat in the back to make sure we didn't fall asleep. On the screen, we saw tabs that organized the different clips: "Overall Play," "Goals For," "Goals Against," and "Set Pieces." Then came the most dreaded: our individual names. Each tab displayed the number of clips it contained. There was always a stomach-dropping moment when you saw this number and thought, "*Wow, I have fourteen lines next to my name, this should be fun.*" I always paired this sarcasm with a positive thought of, "*Well, maybe some of them are good!*" even though I knew the latter was unlikely to be true.

What these clips taught us—other than the ability to take criticism—was the discrepancy between how we *thought* we executed a play, versus how the play *actually* happened. By seeing this gap, we learned how we could improve and be more successful the next time.

Similarly, when Jaz spoke about self-actualization, she indicated we must reflect on our actual thoughts and why we think they are justified in comparison with what's really going on, what our intentions are, and how we're holding ourselves back from where we want to go. In our film of life and retrospection, we must evaluate the gaps between our thoughts and actions to figure out how we can start to close these gaps rather than widen them.

STRONG A** CHICK

Jaz had to learn the idea of self-actualization from a young age because of her experiences as a person of color in the US. She said, "When you're a person of color, your parents have a conversation with you early on about how people will have lower expectations of you and assumptions about how you will fit in." As a Black woman born in Trinidad, she cited her experiences with racism, microaggressions, and macroaggressions when she came to the US.

At the start of her career in fashion, she was the first Black sales executive at Liz Claiborne. She talked on the phone with a woman from Nashville who owned a boutique that carried the Liz Claiborne brand. When the woman came to visit for NYC market week, Jaz walked up to greet her and put her hand out. Without shaking Jaz's hand, the woman said, "I'm here to see Jasmine."

Jaz responded, "I *am* Jasmine." The woman cringed, having clearly thought that the voice with a Brooklyn accent she had heard over the phone belonged to a white woman instead of Jaz, a Black woman. Jaz had been teased as a child since she didn't have an American Black accent, as she was from Trinidad and she went to school in the predominantly Italian-American Park Slope area of Brooklyn.

When Jaz worked as a sales assistant at a major fashion company, the Vice President of Sales told her he was from Louisiana and that he knew about the "Paper Bag Test." Jaz had no idea what that meant, so he explained that if your skin was darker than a paper bag, you couldn't gain entry into social events. He then held a paper bag up to Jaz's face, laughing as he told her she would get in. During their conversation, he also alluded to Jaz liking watermelon and fried chicken, a clear Black stereotype.

When Jaz started her fitness business, clients would often come into her gym asking Jaz if they could speak to the *real* owner when they approached her at the front desk. These were examples of the racist realities about which her parents had warned her. Many people around her felt too uncomfortable to speak up on her behalf and didn't understand the impact their non-actions had on a Black woman who was the only person who looked like her in those rooms.

Jaz said to me, "I'm a strong a** chick. I know that I'm Black. I know that I'm a Black woman. I also know that I also have an edge because people like me. And that's what helped me go from working at Speedo to DKNY to Liz Claiborne and eventually with Jay-Z."

Jaz's gym isn't in on any "Top 10 Gyms in NYC" lists and she doesn't have the most famous influencers taking her classes. But what she does possess is one of the greatest hearts I've ever encountered. She has the power to uplift people regardless of how they arrive in her home, and her passion for others truly elevates her community.

She's a fighter, both for herself and for her people. She will love you whether you're broken or fully healed. She is the first and only Black woman in many situations, and she uses this fact to fuel her purpose. She's a successful entrepreneur who lives with an infectious positive attitude and carries an energy—whether it's in a booty class or saving someone who just quit their job—that leaves you feeling better than when you arrived. All of these components are her unique superpowers, and they are what make her a Superhero.

GENERAL COUNSEL

Often, the key lessons we learn from being the first are lessons that not only help define how we're going to lead, but also become our steadfast values as we rise to prestigious positions.

Maryanne Lavan is the first-ever female Senior Vice President, General Counsel, and Corporate Secretary for the aerospace, defense, arms, security, and advanced technologies company Lockheed Martin. The company makes more than $65 billion in revenue and is number fifty-seven of the Fortune 500 as of 2021.[11] As General Counsel, Maryanne leads the entire legal department for the international company and serves on Lockheed Martin's Executive Leadership Team.

Since she arrived at the company, Maryanne has continued to break boundaries. She was the first female and youngest-ever General Counsel of one of the Lockheed Martin's business areas. Despite her accomplishments, as a child Maryanne didn't imagine she would be the first woman in one of the most prestigious legal positions available. Maryanne told me that growing up as a woman in her generation, "I not only didn't know what I could do, but I almost didn't want to be a smart woman then because smart women were not *typical*."

Maryanne grew up in Farmingdale on Long Island, New York, and was the oldest of seven siblings. Her father was public-school teacher, so naturally, education was the most important thing in her family. Growing up in the lower-middle class, Maryanne went to the most affordable state school she could: State University of New York at Albany. She graduated Magna Cum Laude, then attended law school at the Washington College of Law at American University in Washington, DC. Even with demanding school responsibilities, she worked throughout her entire collegiate career, from the

---

11   "Fortune 500: Lockheed Martin," Fortune 500 Ranking, *Fortune*, updated February 2, 2021.

day she started her undergraduate studies until the day she graduated from law school.

> "I learned the importance of hard work and doing the best at everything I could, whether I was cleaning bathrooms and shoveling sand during my undergraduate summers or working at a distinguished law firm. I had no other options but to do my best."
>
> MARYANNE LAVAN

In her first summer as a new lawyer, Maryanne made more money than her dad had during the year before his retirement. She continued to reflect on how grateful she was that her parents instilled in her the importance of education and hard work and credits her success today to their educational encouragement. As of 2019, Maryanne was one of just 165 female General Counsels in the Fortune 500, up five percent from 2017.[12]

Maryanne's pathway to becoming the first female General Counsel at Lockheed Martin relied on building trust, being resilient in her values, and pulling others up with her.

When Maryanne was newly appointed in her first role as a business area General Counsel, she recalled being the only woman at a table with roughly ten men; at the time, there

---

12 Phillip Bantz, "More Minority, Women General Counsel at Top US Companies than Ever Before," Law: Corporate Counsel, August 31, 2020.

were very few women in the legal department and almost none in legal positions. The executive in charge of the business area talked favorably about all the leaders at the table. Lastly, he looked at Maryanne, the only woman. She started thinking, "Oh my gosh, what is he going say about me? That I have nothing to offer?"

He effectively said, "I want you to know that I rely on Maryanne for legal and contractual advice. If you have legal or contractual issues that need to be solved, you need to go through her first before you come to me." Those words of recognition and support changed the dynamics of the team. In an environment full of men and only one woman, the men recognized that the most senior man in the room saw Maryanne as important, so they were going to treat her as important, too. During that meeting, Maryanne learned the weight that the words of someone in a position of power carried. Maryanne told me, "Trust—especially when you are the only one who looks like you—might take years to build, but when people know you authentically and trust you, they'll work with you."

Throughout her career, she became the person everyone turned to for advice on how to embrace others. Much like her boss who had vouched for her, she made words of recognition and outspoken support and confidence in her people a staple of her leadership style. Maryanne has strived to create environments in which her employees could know her authentically and could feel comfortable bringing their full selves to work. This—along with words of affirmation—has helped her create trust among her employees and colleagues.

"I stand for what I believe in, and I think about what makes for a better business. What goes around comes around. If I can help someone and that person turns around and helps someone else, it makes for a far better world."

MARYANNE LAVAN

In order to use her position as the first woman in many situations to make sure she is not the last, Maryanne said, "I try to recognize people who may not have had all the advantages in the world and help to them to succeed and continue to grow." She has used this mindset to leverage her position as one of the first female General Counsels to pave the way for others.

MADAME VICE PRESIDENT
In November 2020, the United States of America elected California Senator Kamala Harris as Vice President, making her the first woman, African American, and person of Southeast Asian descent to be elected as Vice President.[13]

Vice President Harris graduated from Howard University, one of the most well-known historically black colleges and universities (HBCUs) before receiving her Juris Doctorate (JD) from the University of California, Berkeley. In 2004, Senator Harris became the first person of color elected as District Attorney of San Francisco. She served in this position until 2011, when she became the first woman, African

---

13   Meredith Deliso, "Kamala Harris set to Make History as 1st Woman of Color to be Vice President," *The New York Times*, January 20, 2021.

American, and person of Southeast Asian descent to hold the office of Attorney General in California's history. Then in 2017, she became one of California's two senators.[14]

The number of women—particularly women of color—who are following in her footsteps politically amplify Vice President Harris's unprecedented feats. As of 2021, 142 women will serve in the United States Congress out of the 535 total positions. In other words, women comprise 26.9 percent of Congressional seats. Specifically, twenty-four women will serve in the US Senate, and 118 women will serve in the US House of Representatives.[15] Fifty-two of these women are women of color, four of whom are in the Senate and forty-eight of whom are in the House of Representatives. Thanks to trailblazers like Vice President Harris, women of color make up 9.7 percent of the total members of Congress.[16]

The Reflective Democracy Campaign, a research group that analyzes the demographics of power in the United States, found that from 2014 to 2020, the presence of women of color in the US Congress grew by 44 percent, by 38 percent in State Legislatures, by 19 percent among county officials, and by 46 percent among city officials. The Reflective Democracy Campaign Director, Brenda Choresi Carter, gave a statement after Senator Harris's nomination as Vice President, saying,

---

14 Catherine Kim and Zack Stanton, "55 Things You Need to Know About Kamala Harris," *Politico*, August 11, 2020.

15 Center for American Women and Politics, "Women in the U.S. Congress 2021," *Eagleton Institute of Politics*, Rutgers, The State University of New Jersey, 2021.

16 "Women of Color in Elective Office 2021," *Eagleton Institute of Politics*, Rutgers, The State University of New Jersey, 2021.

"Kamala Harris is not only a historic 'first,' she is representative of a broader truth: the American people are hungry for elected leaders who share their life experiences and perspectives; and when given a chance to vote for them, they will."[17]

When then-Senator Harris received her nomination as presidential candidate Joe Biden's running mate, *The New York Times* captured a number of sentiments from different people. One first-generation Indian American woman described the dichotomy of her excitement about seeing someone who represents her, but also criticism for the ways in which Senator Harris has affected this woman's community:

"Kamala Harris's nomination is meaningful to me. Representation matters, I acknowledge that. But she is nowhere near as far left as people are imagining her to be. Black and Indian women as demographics are far further to the left than she is on many policy topics that, for me, are deal breaking. She means a lot to me and I will proudly vote for her, but I want to acknowledge the ways in which she has harmed working-class (specifically Black working-class) communities." *Divya Bharadwaj, 27, Seattle.*[18]

Sentiments such as Divya's raise a contention—what is more important: seeing diverse representation or not seeing diverse representation due to disagreement with that person's values and history? We try to make this question simple, as if it is one or the other, but the truth is, the answer is incredibly

---

17   Brenda Choresi Carter, "Seeking Reflective Leadership, Voters Elect Kamala Harris," *Reflective Democracy Campaign*, November 7, 2020.

18   Rachel L. Harris, "Kamala Harris's Nomination Is Everything to Me," *The New York Times*, August 15, 2020.

nuanced. In some versions of Vice President Harris's story, she is cast as the hero, achieving unparalleled positions for women of color.

With regard to criminal justice reform during her time as Attorney General of California, Senator Harris is cast as a villain, criticized by the disconnect between her actions and confusing messaging, as she labelled herself "California's Top Cop."[19] In positions as prominent as Vice President Harris's, she is subject to—and I believe rightfully so—criticism from every angle. But what dilemma Vice President Harris's nomination particularly raises is our obsession with labeling people—especially people in positions of power—as heroes, victims, or villains. We also have an obsession with categorizing women—especially women of color—who might operate differently than how the world expects women to behave, regardless of their power.

We need to abolish the categories into which we have shoved women; we need to be become comfortable with seeing a leader who does not look like us or what we are accustomed to seeing. We need to reevaluate what is most important to our personal values no matter the skin tone of our leaders. We need to re-create structures so women of color have the same opportunities as white women and so all women have the same opportunities as men.

---

19 Nicholas Reimann, "Biden Picked A 'Cop': Some on Left Slam Choice Of Kamala Harris For VP," *Forbes*, August 11, 2020.

UNBURDENED, UNWAVERING, UNDAUNTED

In October of 2018, then-Senator Kamala Harris gave a speech to Spelman University. Spelman University started in the basement of a church, and now, over a century later, is the top ranked HBCU in the country.[20]

In her speech, she said, "My mother would look at me and she'd say, 'Kamala you may be the first to do many things, but make sure you are not the last.'" She continued, "... that's why breaking those barriers is worth it. As much as anything else, it is also to create that path for those who will come after us."[21]

Harris cited some of her experiences being the only women of color in the courtroom or in the Senate hearing room. She pointed out that even though prestigious Spelman students would find themselves in many situations where they were the only person of color, it's "critically important" they remembered they were not alone. They were part of a broader family, and not just within Spelman. Then-Senator Harris closed her speech with:

---

20   "Historically Black Colleges and Universities," Best Colleges: US News & World Report Rankings, *US News*, updated 2021.

21   Kamala Harris, "Undaunted by the Fight," (lecture, Spelman College, Atlanta, Georgia, October 26, 2018).

"Whatever the future holds, toil and pain, know that you can walk into any situation, you can lead in any field, you can take on any challenge, and you will go forward unburdened, unwavering, and undaunted by the fight."[22]

KAMALA HARRIS

The truth is, at any given moment, we can be any of these—a hero, a victim, or a villain. Most leaders are acting with their gut instincts and their gained knowledge of the world. We are disillusioned to believe people can be 100 percent hero all of the time and that everyone will agree with our decisions.

We must also ask if we are more inclined to judge the first representation of someone we see more harshly than someone we are used to? Are we more inclined to scrutinize Vice President Harris's actions because she is one of the first women of color we have seen in those positions of power she has held?

In the nearly twenty-five decades that have passed since the United States officially became an independent country in 1776, we have never had a woman serve in the most powerful position in the country—the presidency—yet women account for 50.8 percent of the US population.[23] After so many years, we finally have a woman—a woman of color, nonetheless—in

22   Ibid.
23   "Quick Facts, by Age and Sex," U.S. Census Bureau, accessed January 27, 2021.

the second most prestigious position in our country. We are getting there slowly, but we still have a long way to go.

Vice President Harris's power may look different from anything we've ever seen. The way she handles situations may look different, but it's on us to not judge her by the low standards we have set for women intellectually or the high standards by which we have judged their physical appearance and silenced them.

To the women who were and are the first, thank you. I can't imagine how difficult it was and still is to be alone. You conquered treacherous mountains with conditions that made it easy to fall off or surrender.

Jasmine Graham, Maryanne Lavan, and Kamala Harris are doing groundbreaking work, each exercising their own superpowers to put themselves in a position of power and representation. Jaz, Kamala, and Maryanne never took "no" for an answer; they kept climbing their mountains, regardless of the conditions and the risks. They continue to construct a trail behind them for people like you and me, and they teach us that we must stand together as teammates, outstretch our arms, and pull one another up. It is our duty to build a pathway for all women at the bottom of treacherous mountains.

CHAPTER 4

YOU SEEING YOU

MERMAIDS

"What do you want to be when you grow up?"

I used to tell anyone who asked, "I'm going to be a mermaid," at least until two of my classmates in Mrs. Delino's first grade class made fun of me and told me it wasn't possible. "No one has ever seen a mermaid before. You can't be one," they teased. As if *they* could tell me what I was going to be when I grew up! I let go of my mermaid fantasy because they were right—I had never seen a mermaid—and I didn't want people to laugh at me.

As I grew older, I realized growing gills seemed even less impossible than having a woman as a United States Supreme Court Justice, the United States Vice President, or even a CEO. I came to learn the bounds of societies—the ones that loudly seemed to tell me what I was and what I was not, and those that silently filled up a room, whispering, *"You're not supposed to be here."* I know these bounds well. They make me feel like a robber taking up someone else's space or causing mischief. I know when I'm in a group that doesn't want me or someone else like me.

When I wanted to be a mermaid, I lived in a wonderful state of bliss. Maybe it was naïveté; I wasn't mature enough to know what was practical or not. However, wanting to be a mermaid was an oasis for me because I didn't confine myself to the bounds I saw. Instead, I explored the furthest my imagination would take me.

Back then, I didn't have rules that made me feel as though I was navigating a maze with walls of thorns poking me until I chose the correct, predestined path. As I grew up, I walked into this maze. Its walls of thorns scaled so high that I couldn't even imagine climbing over them, and the pathway in front of me seemed filled with a low-hanging fog that sent chills up my spine. I looked down to catch my footing, unable to see ahead.

I thought this maze predetermined my destiny and what I was *supposed* to be versus what I *wanted* to be. I thought that on the outside of the maze, onlookers saw magnificent, bold petals. However, on the inside of this maze, the rose thorns pierced me and controlled me like a shock collar anytime I tried to step off of the path.

Those rose thorns pierced my mermaid-scaled flesh as I bounced back and forth between the walls, feeling unfit for the life I saw ahead of me and unable to see myself in the people this maze predetermined me to be like. My gaze stayed down as I narrowed my focus on each individual step, trying desperately to find fulfillment in what I could control and too disheartened to wonder what the fog was hiding.

I asked myself, *"Do I continue walking this maze and risk suffering an unfulfilled life if I reach the end? Or do I navigate through the walls filled with thorns that could cause me to bleed to death and fog that could encapsulate me, for the opportunity to have what I truly want?"*

This is what the first female schoolteacher, doctor, lawyer, entrepreneur, professional athlete, and C-suite executive must have asked themselves. This is what all females who have never seen a woman in the role they desire must have felt like.

It is because of these *first* women that I and so many other women have found the courage to peek through the rose thorns, see someone who represents us, and know we can actualize our mermaid dreams—the ones we had when we knew no bounds.

RUSTY RIMS

Representation allows us to see the art of the possible and reimagine what our futures could hold. Have you ever said to yourself, "I know I can do it because I see *her* doing it?"

I met my friend, Dyzhanay "Didi" Burton, while we were both student-athletes at Georgetown University. Growing up in poverty-stricken neighborhoods of Baltimore, Maryland, with high crime, Didi sought refuge in basketball.

Starting in middle school, when the chaos at home enveloped her, she headed straight to the outdoor basketball court, shoveling snow or bearing the extreme summer heat to shoot at a hoop with a rusted rim and no net.

It wasn't until Didi saw what basketball had done for her neighbor, La'Shay Taft, who lived across the courtyard from her nearly her whole life, that Didi realized it could take her out of her predestined future on the streets—her personal rose thorn maze. La'Shay was recruited to an exceptional club basketball team program in New York and eventually went on to play for the Syracuse University Women's Basketball program. She became a mentor to Didi and, most importantly, gave Didi the confidence that she had the ability to use basketball as her ticket to college. La'Shay was one of the first people Didi told after she had accepted a full-ride scholarship from Georgetown University's Women's Basketball Team.

For the majority of high school, Didi slept a total of four hours every night. She woke up early to take three buses to school where she attended morning workouts followed by class all day, then headed straight to afternoon practice. After practice, she went to her to her old math teacher's classroom where she would do her homework because she didn't have a computer at home, let alone Wi-Fi. Her math teacher, who helped her apply for college, would drive her home in the late hours of the night. She repeated this process every day until she arrived on campus at Georgetown.

"Where I'm from, a lot of odds are stacked against you based on a history of compounded disadvantages.

It means a lot when people make it out of Baltimore and make something out of nothing."

DYZHANAY BURTON

Didi told me, "Now, on my street in Washington, DC, when I want to blow off some steam or I want to go have fun, I have access to three different gyms, a juice bar, and a bike share program to ride around the city—I have only healthy options to choose from, no matter what mood I'm in."

Because Didi had a front-row seat to La'Shay's collegiate career through basketball, Didi was able to construct a new future for herself. She recalled the day she stepped onto Georgetown's campus—also known as the Hilltop—a week before her freshman year. Though Georgetown was only an hour and a half away from her hometown, she had never visited because she didn't have easy access to travel there. She looked out from the Hilltop and in the direction of Baltimore with an equal admiration for where she had come from and where she had arrived. This hilltop that Didi had climbed was not an accident, and it became possible because of women like La'Shay who had shown her the path to the top. It was never that Georgetown was better than Baltimore; it was that Georgetown had the resources to endlessly support Didi and her dreams. Didi continues to be incredibly grateful for where she has come from and where she has gone, and she is making it her life mission to help others have a shot at pursuing the life they envision for themselves.

Throughout her journey, Didi has taken hardships in stride every single day. When Didi was a senior in college, she had to make the preparations for her father's funeral. In fall 2020, she became one of the caregivers for her three-year-old niece after walking in on her sister's suicide. Though she has experienced inconceivable loss, she has never let herself act as a victim. Instead, she has always turned hardship into opportunities, whether it was going to the court to practice her game in middle school or giving back to her Baltimore community as she does now. In 2019, Didi started a company called "ABG Elite Homes, LLC" in hopes of restoring community centers for children and adults to play. Her dream is for Baltimore to one day have more parks and community centers—more places that provide opportunities for hope and bring out the best in the city and its people.

The power of representation allows us to see the superpowers within ourselves so that when we embark on a hill, we can make it to the top.

Representation comes in people of all ages, backgrounds, and industries. By being in a visible position for others like you, you can give others the courage to burn down their thorn walls and rebuild a garden for future women to enjoy.

When it comes to representation, seeing is believing.

SEEING IS BELIEVING

The sports industry has the potential to become one of the most highly visible platforms for women's representation. Unfortunately, women's professional sports coverage currently only represents 4 percent of all sports media, just 3 percent higher from 1994.[24] It's not that women aren't playing sports—it's that the media doesn't show them. The biggest source of financial support for sports leagues, teams, and athletes comes from media contracts and brand sponsorships that increase their collective visibility. Because sports media barely exhibits women's collegiate and professional sports, women's sports leagues and teams lack the financial resources necessary to sustain their presence and grow.

The sports industry, forecasted to be valued at $614.1 billion in 2022, has grown nearly 6 percent in the last three years, largely due to additional media outlets such as social media.[25] Media allows people to not only spectate sports in more convenient ways, but it also allows them to build relationships with their favorite teams and athletes. When the media don't visually represent women athletes, it suggests to the world that women athletes don't matter and that women's sports aren't as important as men's sports. Furthermore, when girls and women don't see themselves visually represented, they are less inclined to believe they can dream of—let alone work toward—a career in sports, or any job for that matter.

---

24 Shira Springer, "7 Ways to Improve Coverage of Women's Sports," *Nieman Reports*, January 7, 2019.
25 "Sports - $614 Billion Global Market Opportunities & Strategies to 2022 - ResearchAndMarkets.com," *Businesswire*, updated May 14, 2019.

Women's fight to earn equality in sports secured a major win in 1972 with the enforcement of the Title IX Education Amendment, which forbid athletic programs at institutions that receive federal funds from discriminating based on gender.[26] Following Title IX, collegiate athletic programs were legally obligated to fund women's and men's athletic teams equally. As a result, not only were more women given greater opportunities to play sports in college, but also more women were able to even *go* to college because they played a sport.[27] Sports helped women pay for college and gave them an edge on their applications when they otherwise would've been overlooked because their qualifications didn't outshine those of the male applicants.

Regardless of whether or not you were a woman who played a sport, Title IX initiated the precedent that women and men are equal, and it served as a huge step toward putting women in visible positions on the field, in the gym, and on the track. Sports continue to be a visual representation of that equality and are important not just at the professional level but also at the youth level.

A small example of this is the uptick in girls' sports participation in Minnesota. As of 2019, Minnesota reported that 49 percent of the state's high school athletes were girls, the highest recorded number of any state. The national average that year for girls' participation in high school sports was 42.7 percent. Minnesota's high percentage was a result of three factors: representation, support, and resources. The WNBA's

26 "Title IX Enacted," *History.com*, accessed March 1, 2021.
27 "Bridging the Gender Gap: The Positive Effects of Title IX," *Athnet: Get Recruited to Play College Sports*, date accessed March 1, 2021.

Minnesota Lynx were highly involved in the state's youth sports, schools offered a higher-than-average number of girls' sports, and there was broad support and appreciation for equality in girls' sports at all levels and ages.[28]

In January 2020, Haley Rosen founded Just Women's Sports, a women's sports media company whose mission is to increase the 4 percent media coverage of women's sports. Haley achieved the pinnacles of success in sports, winning a NCAA Championship at Stanford University, playing professional soccer in the US National Women's Soccer League (NWSL) for the Washington Spirit, and finishing her professional soccer career in Europe. During her career, her games were often sold out and people waited for hours after the game to engage with their favorite athletes. "I felt the momentum of women's sports," Haley told me.

It wasn't until Haley retired from soccer that she started to really notice the 4 percent media coverage of women's sports. She wanted to follow women's sports, watch highlights, hear about trades, rivalries, and game analysis, but she couldn't find this coverage anywhere.

Upon realizing this gap, Haley created an Instagram account called Just Women's Sports to amplify the voices and playing abilities of female athletes. The account started growing quickly, and Haley said that "[the quick growth] was such validation. I didn't have any tricks because I wasn't an expert in social media or Instagram." From there, Haley officially

---

28 Bob Cook, "Inside the Numbers on Girls' Participation in High School Sports," Lifestyle (blog), *Forbes*, March 30, 2019.

launched her company Just Women's Sports (JWS) and debuted a podcast hosted by US Women's Team player and fellow Stanford University Women's Soccer alumna, Kelley O'Hara. Kelley is a three-time World Cup Champion, a Hermann Trophy Winner—an award given to the best college soccer player—and regarded as one of the best defenders in the world.[29]

In its inaugural week, iTunes ranked the *JWS* podcast as the number one sports podcast, determined by the velocity of streams. Since its debut, the podcast has hosted some of the best female athletes ever to play their sports, including basketball's Candace Parker, soccer's Alex Morgan, and snowboarding's Chloe Kim. In addition to the successes and setbacks that many of these athletes share, as a child, all of them saw someone who they wanted to be like.

"From a young age, every single one of these top athletes we highlight saw someone who moved like them or was a representation of them at the highest level. It continues to drive home for me that you have to see it to be it. I cannot emphasize that enough."

HALEY ROSEN

Just Women's Sports exclusively covers women's sports news, including league updates, team trades, and game highlights, as well as financial and social equality in women's sports.

---

29 "Kelley O'Hara," US Soccer: Kelley O'Hara. *USWNT.* February 15, 2021.

Their profound and compelling sports stories are setting the precedent for sports coverage for media companies who have traditionally covered women's sports through a surface-level and materialistic lens. Rather than talking about an athlete's style of hair, Just Women's Sports wants to talk about her style of play. This approach not only emphasizes that female athletes should be taken more seriously, but also that women should be taken more seriously in general. Haley said, "We're focusing on sports and building gender equality through sports. But through women's sports, our greater hope is to achieve greater equality more broadly."

Amplifying women's sports media is an avenue that can help us see women in places we didn't know were possible doing things we didn't think were possible. The women's sports industry is a visible microcosm demonstrating how women can achieve gender equality not just in the workplace but also in our communities and social structures at large.

BREAKING THROUGH

Maybe you personally feel like there's no hope of escaping your rose thorn maze, but I encourage you to think of Didi and Haley. Maybe you'll see an opportunity to amplify the equality of women and their talents through a mechanism like sports.

For a moment, channel your younger self and ask yourself honestly, *"Without bounds or limits, what do I want to be when I grow up?"* Then, go find someone who looks like you, one person who believes in you, and one resource you can use to get there.

Representation, support, and resources.

Break through your rose thorn wall and go after who you want to be. Remember, *you seeing you* can save your life. And maybe one day, them seeing you can save theirs.

PART 2

AWAKEN YOUR SUPERPOWERS

CHAPTER 5

CHOOSE YOUR FIGHT

In order to truly awaken your superpowers, you must first understand the people and the causes for which you choose to fight. Once you recognize the cyclical effects of Superheroism like Miss Val described, you will begin to see how fighting for others on a deeper level also brings out the best in you. Two of my Superheroes—former Supreme Court Justice, Ruth Bader Ginsburg (RBG) and my former coach, Lyndse Hokanson—both fought for others through two different avenues—one in the Highest Court of the Land and the other on a soccer field. However, through both RBG's and Lyndse's fights, I discovered that we cannot neglect combating our own inner monsters. We must take what they teach us and apply it to our life's mission and the causes and people for which we choose to fight, including ourselves.

RUTH BADER GINSBURG
Famous women's rights activist, Gloria Steinem, said in 2018, "[Ruth Bader Ginsburg] is the closest thing to a Superhero

I know."[30] For her entire life, RBG never stopped fighting for the rights of others, regardless of race, gender, ethnicity, age, or disability. It is my intention to share her lifelong fight so that we may be filled with gratitude and understand the dedication needed to embark on our own Superhero journeys.

On Friday, September 18, 2020, I was dining outdoors at a Spanish tapas restaurant celebrating a college soccer teammate's birthday. We laughed through our masks and smiled with our eyes, only pulling our masks down to sip sangria and eat paella. Just under three miles away from the United States Supreme Court, we let ourselves enjoy the night and one another's company—something that had been rare during the last seven months we had all spent trapped in the COVID-19 pandemic. We felt lucky to have the means to eat out while so many others were suffering.

"Oh my gosh!" my friend Arielle said in a somber tone that we had all seemed to become uncomfortably accustomed to. I knew someone had just died.

"What happened?" I asked Arielle. "RBG just died," she remarked in disbelief. We all immediately grabbed our phones and loaded our social media applications. Our news feeds were flooded with outcries and bewilderment. People were trying to grasp how the dear Supreme Court Justice and warrior for human rights, Ruth Bader Ginsburg, was now gone forever. The mood at our dinner turned into devastation. The jovial atmosphere around us changed drastically,

---

30 Naz Beheshti, "5 Timely Leadership Lessons From 'R.B.G.': The Oscar-Nominated Documentary About Ruth Bader Ginsberg," *Forbes*, March 28, 2019.

as if the lead singer at a concert had just fallen off the stage. The laughter and chatter all around us turned to whispers as hands covered mouths and wet cheeks glistened on almost every woman I saw under the restaurant's lights.

After we finished eating, the waiter handed us our check. Our respective credit cards sat neatly in our wallets, waiting to be swiped. RBG was the reason we had credit cards. She helped enact the Equal Credit Opportunity Act in 1974 which "prohibit[ed] discrimination on the basis of race, color, religion, national origin, sex, marital status, or age in credit transactions."[31]

Because we had credit cards, we could earn credit, which meant we could put a down payment on a car or a house. It meant we could gather for meals with our best friends and share memories. It meant we could invest and accrue wealth. It meant we could take risks with our careers and be the breadwinners. It meant we could afford to raise a family or choose not to. We had the power to decide *our* lives for *ourselves*.

RBG didn't officially serve on a federal bench until 1980, but she won a significant number of cases related to equality prior to then. In 1971, she won the case Reed v. Reed, one of RBG's six landmark case wins before being nominated to the Supreme Court in 1993 by President Bill Clinton. RBG co-authored the brief for this case which argued that "a provision of Idaho state law, saying men were to be preferred to women

---

31 Samantha Rosen, "How Ruth Bader Ginsburg Paved the Way for Women to Get Credit Cards," *Time,* November 13, 2020.

in appointing the administrators of an estate," violated the Constitution.[32] The court agreed with RBG's brief and found unanimously that incongruent treatment "on the basis of sex" between women and men "was unconstitutional." The National Women's Law Center said the verdict "marked the first time in history that the Court applied the Equal Protection Clause of the Fourteenth Amendment to strike down a law that discriminated against women."[33]

RBG, originally named Joan Ruth Bader, was born on March 15, 1933 in Brooklyn, New York, during the height of the Great Depression. Her father worked as a furrier—someone who prepared furs—and her mother worked in a garment factory. RBG's mother had a tremendous impact on her, but unfortunately passed away from breast cancer on the day of RBG's high school graduation.[34]

RBG attended the Ivy League school Cornell University and graduated at the top of her class in 1954, just before marrying her husband, Martin. Two years after her college graduation, RBG had her daughter and the military drafted Martin. When Martin returned two years later, he enrolled at Harvard Law, and RBG followed in his footsteps the next year. RBG was one of nine women in her class of five hundred at Harvard Law.

During her first year of law school, Martin was diagnosed with testicular cancer. RBG took care of her husband's health,

---

32   Ibid.
33   Ibid
34   Ibid.

attended *his* law classes, attended *her* law classes, and cared for their toddler. All the while, RBG faced tremendous gender-based discrimination, especially from male executives at Harvard; the dean of Harvard Law school hosted a "Lady's Dinner" and invited all of the first-year women, only to ask them why they were taking a seat meant for a man.[35] Despite all of these hardships, RBG continued to prove the naysayers wrong and became the first female member of the *Harvard Law Review.*

Martin recovered from cancer in time to graduate and took a job in New York City. RBG decided to follow Martin and transferred to Columbia University Law School where she would graduate first in her class in 1959. She would later become Columbia Law School's first tenured female law professor.[36]

My friends and I walked home after dinner that night close to Georgetown University, where we had all met and played soccer together. Sixty years prior, we wouldn't have been allowed to attend Georgetown. Just eighteen years prior, Georgetown didn't even have funding for a Women's Soccer program.

That night, we rejoiced in our Sisterhood, acknowledging how lucky we were because of the women who came before us. We wouldn't have had the accomplishments, memories, experiences, and resulting opportunities had it not been for women like RBG. She opened up doors for

---

35 "Ruth Bader Ginsburg," *Oyez*, accessed January 28, 2021.
36 Ibid.

us so that we could stretch our dreams and imaginations and helped us gain entry into rooms we once were not allowed to enter.

Walking home that night, we were also afraid; RBG had protected our bodies and our right to control them as we saw best fit. We asked each other when we had last seen our gynecologists and whether or not we had enough birth control and other necessities just in case our bodily rights would be stripped in the aftermath of her death. We were family planning and protecting one another. We looked out for each other like sisters, just like RBG did for us.

We let ourselves grieve that night. Thereafter, we knew we had to fight for ourselves, for our Sisterhood, for LGBTQ members, and for anyone who faced discrimination. We knew it was our duty to carry RBG's torch of equality, respect, and justice and to keep the flame forever burning.

My favorite quote by RBG is "Fight for the things that you care about, but do it in a way that will lead others to join you."

For whom and what will *you* fight?

FIGHTING YOUR MONSTER

In order for us to answer this question, we need to first understand and combat our inner monsters that prohibit us from doing our Superhero work.

For anyone who played a fall sport in college, you know the middle of the summer is preseason—arguably the most dreaded yet most coveted time in sports. Preseason is the ultimate test of physical, mental, and emotional fitness. How hard can you push yourself until you crack? It's also the start of a new season, when aspirations for winning your league championship keep you sprinting even when you're on the verge of throwing up or collapsing from exhaustion. In Washington, DC, the summer heat tops 100 degrees with 95 percent humidity. It's a perfect breeding ground for mosquitoes and being out on the field feels like you've just jumped into a hot, dirty lake—you're swollen, smelly, and uncomfortably soaked.

It was 7:15 a.m. in August on a beautiful, swampy day, and we had just finished conditioning practice. I picked up the cones that marked our sprint lines, trying to hide the tears welling up in my eyes. We were in our third week of the season and had three games under our belts. It was my fifth year on the Georgetown Women's Soccer team and my third year as captain. Up until this point in my career, I had started and played almost every minute of every game. That is, until I medically red-shirted my senior year. Red-shirting means you forgo that season of playing due to an injury or other circumstance, but you can bank that year for an additional year of playing eligibility as long as your total doesn't exceed four seasons. This was my comeback season after tearing my ACL twice in nine months and being in physical—and let's be honest, mental—rehabilitation for two years. All I wanted was for things to return to normal— to feel athletic again, to attack the game with tenacity and poise, to compete against the top teams in the country, and to win championships without worrying about my knee collapsing at any moment.

I wanted to play so badly that I was unable to see I wasn't ready to play. I looked like Bambi on ice: running in circles without any coordination. Though I had the memory of how I *used* to move and react, my muscles and new knee were still being re-trained how to follow.

The pressure of leading my hyper-driven teammates when I was prideful and unready to play completely overwhelmed me. Soccer gave me everything: my lifelong friends, a path to one of the best universities in the country, confidence, and passion. When I couldn't play the way I used to, I was miserable. I was a horrible teammate during those weeks and—even worse—a destructive leader. I didn't cheer for my teammates when they scored or didn't give a compelling pre-game speech. I was drowning in my own pity party all around me. I took the self-hatred boiling up inside me and imposed it upon my teammates.

I didn't realize how much of monster I could become until I was broken down physically, mentally, and emotionally. I also didn't know what I was capable of until I hit rock bottom, gained perspective, and emerged from the pounds of gravel I felt buried under. The difference between spiraling further into the ground versus climbing out from under the cement rocks was a decision I made to choose my team over myself.

This is what Lyndse Hokanson, my assistant coach at the time, taught me on that swampy morning when the lacrosse-sized ball of frustration in my chest made the quarter-sized mosquito bites on my legs feel soothing.

She pulled me aside and said, "What's going on?"

"You know what's going on," I retorted. "I'm f***ing miserable because I'm not playing, and I should be. Why did I work my a** off to come back from two destructive knee injuries just to not play? I never should have come back."

"No," she said. "What's going on with you in your head? This person isn't you. And on top of that, you are single-handedly destroying this team. You need to understand that in your position as captain, you're the binding between the coaches and the players. You're the one with the most experience with Georgetown Soccer. Your *leadership* means far more than your playing ability. You need to get over the fact that you aren't playing, and you need to start bringing out the best in this team. Don't make a decision that ruins your teams' season and that you'll regret for the rest of your life."

My gaze drifted from her eyes to the wet grass. My lips were pursed and my tears stung my eyes, partly out of frustration but mostly from realizing that she was right.

"Leadership means more than your playing ability."

Injuries happen to every human on this planet. Some of us experience physical injuries through sports and others through heartbreak, disease, or genetics. Our inner monsters falsely tell us that we aren't worthy of anything until we fix these injuries. When my knee was fixed, I thought I would return, unbroken. It turns out that my biggest injury of all was my deep-rooted perfectionism. It told me I had to be a certain way, and when I couldn't be, I shut down.

Lyndse had one more suggestion for me before she left the field and allowed me to sit with my thoughts on Shaw Field, the Georgetown University soccer field and the one place on Earth I felt the most myself. She said, "Kid, look at your teammates who rarely play in games. Have you ever noticed them in practice? They're the hardest working players on our team and have some of the best attitudes. You need to start being honest with yourself not about the soccer player you want to be but about the *person* you want to be when things don't go your way. You need to be happy and proud again of the person looking back at you in the mirror." I couldn't tell you the last time I had felt proud of myself before Lyndse said that. All I knew was that I wasn't perfect and that imperfection slowly sliced my flesh like paper cuts, eventually reaching my fragile soul.

Perfectionism is still my inner monster I battle every day, but that conversation with Lyndse fundamentally changed my life. It changed the way I approached myself, the way I approached being a part of a team, and the way I approached leadership.

Coming out of this moment, there were three things I specifically knew I needed to learn:

- I couldn't lead others without taking ownership of my own actions and becoming the leader of my own life.
- I needed to spend more time listening, especially to my teammates and to my coaches.
- I needed to leave everyone better than I found them and live every day with passion.

I didn't have control over my injury, but I had the power to choose how I wanted this unfortunate situation to turn out. I could choose for whom and what I wanted to fight. And so do you.

> "Whether you like it or not, everybody is looking at you in good times and bad. What are they seeing?"
>
> LYNDSE HOKANSON

How was I going to take these leadership opportunities, fight my inner monster, and make a positive impact? The first thing I did was become extra observant of my teammates who didn't start in games or those who never played. I also worked to unlearn my childish and selfish behavior and re-learn the fundamentals of being a good teammate: working hard, emitting positive energy, constantly moving the joint mission forward, and having fun. I missed having fun.

During the fifth game of our season, my teammate got injured, so I went in at center back, my old defensive position. I never came off the field for the rest of the season. I constantly worked on the way I treated myself, the way I treated my teammates and everyone to whom I talked, and humbly developed into a leader again.

That year, we became Georgetown's best Women's Soccer team ever. We won the championship in our league, the Big East, for the first time. We made it to the NCAA College Cup Final Four for the first time. We ranked number three in the country, our highest ranking ever. We solidified ourselves as one of the best soccer programs in the nation, and our team's success has sustained, if not improved, ever since.

PRESSURE TESTS

I would be remiss to say that our success was purely due to talent, because it was far from that. Yes, we had talent—you have to at that level. But what made us excel started with Lyndse's Superhero leadership that allowed us to play the game we loved freely and with passion. Every day, on campus or at practice, Lyndse made sure everyone on the team felt seen and important.

Before Lyndse Hokanson arrived at Georgetown University, the women's soccer program consistently ranked in the Top 25 nationally but had only once broken the threshold into the Elite 8 of teams. We had the skill caliber of a Top 15 program, but we lacked the buy-in, team camaraderie, and passion to make it to the top. Everything changed when Lyndse helped teach us to choose our team over ourselves.

Lyndse and I recounted our conversation on Shaw Field and our 2016 season four years later. She said, "The purpose that I found for myself as an assistant coach during our then-most successful season ever at Georgetown Women's Soccer was to make sure every single person on that team felt like they had value. That piece of leadership—seeing people, hearing them, and caring for them—is what guides the rest of it."

Lyndse was the starting goalkeeper for the George Mason Women's Soccer team and graduated in 2014. When Lyndse arrived at George Mason, she foresaw a career in Sports Journalism. After she coached a soccer camp during the summer before her junior year and worked with Nicole, a fourteen-year-old girl who had never played soccer before, she realized her passion and purpose was to coach. The camp was for elite soccer players who had aspirations to play in college, but Nicole's parents signed Nicole up just so she'd have something to do.

On the last night of the camp, Lyndse set up a goalkeeper pressure training test—a very intense set of training circuits designed to evaluate the goalkeeper's fitness and skillset. Lyndse had two rules for her goalkeepers for this test: athletes couldn't say the word "can't" and once you start, you can't stop.

She said, "Once you start the training, you finish your rep and get back up onto your feet because as goalkeepers, we can't show weakness."

Nicole started her pressure test, and it quickly became extremely difficult for her. After making it more than halfway through, Nicole dropped to all fours. Lyndse gave the group a water break and went over to Nicole. She asked, "Are you okay?"

Nicole stared at the ground and said, "Just give me a second."

"You can stop if you want to," Lyndse offered, worried about Nicole's lack of playing experience and, as a result, lack of fitness.

"No, I'm not going to stop," Nicole replied. "I want to finish. Just give me a second to catch my breath." Shortly after, Nicole got up and finished the entire pressure test.

That night, as the coaches and players were sitting in the lobby of the athletic facility, Nicole came and sat down next to Lyndse.

Lyndse asked, "How are you doing?"

Nicole replied, "I'm really tired and I'm really sore, but I just wanted to say thank you. That was the hardest I've ever been pushed, and you made me believe I could finish it."

Reflecting back on that moment, Lyndse told me:

"That was the moment in my life I recognized the impact you can have on a kid's life as a coach. I could look into Nicole's eyes and see that she felt valued and believed in. She felt like she could do something she didn't think she could do walking into that camp."

LYNDSE HOKANSON

From that moment, Lyndse began her coaching career and never looked back. She started coaching at the club level before moving to high school. Eventually, she coached at Valdosta State before landing at Georgetown University. Recently, she's become the head coach at Colgate University.

SPRINKLES OF SUPERHERO LEADERSHIP

Lyndse defines Superhero Leadership as pushing people to show them who they can be, loving them enough to allow them to fail, then picking them back up and continuing to push them forward. She centers her leadership style around individual connection and always being exactly who she is. She took the weight off of my shoulders to be perfect and, instead, helped me learn I had the space to be myself—emotional, passionate, goofy, loud, quirky, and bold. She taught me that through my individuality, I could become not just an incredible athlete, but also manifest into my unique person.

With regards to coaching and leading, Lyndse told me, "You can't do the teaching and the growing until you do the loving. That looks like developing skills on the field as much as it means texting you when I have nachos and all I can think about is the mountain of salsa you put on everything. It's about immersing yourself into the lives of the kids that you're trying to teach and grow."

She continued, "That's the gift I bring to the job, and if I ever feel as though I'm not doing that anymore, then I need to find a new job." Lyndse is a championship coach who has achieved success through motivation, love, and truly seeing her players. She transformed the way we looked at ourselves and the way we looked at one another.

RBG and Lyndse's individual and unique styles of fight have transformed lives in their own individual ways. You don't need to be a Supreme Court Justice or a National Coach of the Year to fight for yourself and others and to impact lives. Instead, RBG and Lynsde show us how Superheroism isn't necessarily about the title we achieve; it's about the people we can help, including ourselves. In our fights we find our Superheroism, and as a result, our titles become a reflection of our fights.

Throughout life, we're given our own individual versions of pressure tests—moments when we're forced to make many micro decisions like choosing to have a good attitude in specific situations, that set the tone for the rest of our lives. Pressure tests measure the resilience of our values, our character, and often, how willing we are to fight our inner monsters. We choose to continue, despite the fact that we might experience something unexpected or encounter interference with our perfect plan. These pressure tests help us discover that we can put in the work to continue to overcome our monsters every day. Though we are never done with the fight to uncover our best selves, discovering the vulnerability within ourselves is the key to resonating with the lives we touch and, ultimately, determine the people and causes for which we choose to fight.

CHAPTER 6

BELIEVE YOUR WORTH

———

TRIGGER WARNING

Some sections in this chapter deal with potentially triggering topics including mental illness and self-harm. Please be aware of this before and as you read. My intention is to share my experiences so they may be helpful in the context of the book and my journey.

In order to make this chapter more accessible for survivors of mental health and self-harm, sections containing direct mention of or the allusion of such topics have a separator between the title and the text.

TRYING TO *BE TOUGH*

Attempting to jump a curb on my bike was the first time I remember feeling the fear of failure and the embarrassment of not being able to do something. My big brother was leading our street's pack of kids as we rode our bikes around the cul-de-sac. I had yet to hop up a curb on my bike out of fear that my front tire wouldn't clear the cement step. I was the only girl in the group—"Chris's Little Sister"—which made me feel like I had something to prove. I thought, *"If I can hop a curb on my bike, I won't be selected last during our street sports games anymore."* So, during my eighth year on Earth, I decided I was going to hop the curb.

I asked my brother to show me once more, though I had memorized his every move. He willingly showed me and asked me again, "Marines, are you sure you're ready?" I could sense the four other neighborhood boys watching doubtfully behind me. I was happy my thick, messy braid draped over my shoulder blocked their disparaging faces; I needed all the confidence I could muster. I nodded my head yes, focused my gaze on the top of the curb seven feet away, and pedaled hard.

My brother shouted, "Handlebars! Pull up your handlebars up!" I tried as hard as I could to pull them up, but it felt like my bike tire was tethered to the ground. My front tire collided with the middle of the curb and I flew over my handlebars, diving face-first onto the cement and crushing my nose. Thankfully, nothing broke except for my neighbors' eardrums as I shrieked with shock and pain, blood streaming onto the light grey cement. My brother screamed, "Marina!" then biked home to get my dad. A few moments later, my dad sprinted down the street. He held my head in his hands and tenderly held his shirt to my nose to stop the bleeding.

He carried me home, set me on the couch with ice and a towel, and asked what I was trying to do in a concerned but not angry tone. *"Be tough,"* my inner voice whispered, as I tried to stop crying, but the pain and embarrassment made not crying impossible. All I wanted was to *be tough* and compartmentalize the pain.

VULNERABILITY AND CONNECTION

Fourteen years later, I still struggle with my inner self-talk. Being tough helped me overcome physical and emotional wounds and, most importantly, taught me to never give up. But trying to be tough also made me believe I had to *earn* happiness instead of waking up and knowing I'm *worthy* of happiness.

Renowned researcher, social worker, and doctor Brené Brown says that when we feel like we have to earn our worth, we're really just "numbing vulnerability." She said people can't select to feel certain emotions and numb others. Doing this negates the positive emotions such as joy, compassion, and gratitude that come along with being vulnerable.[37] This happens when we experience failure or setbacks; when we compartmentalize the pain of crashing into a curb, we also compartmentalize the love we receive when someone rests our head in their hands and stops the bleeding.

Brené Brown also says the one thing every social worker knows to be true is that everybody needs connection and the ability to feel connected. "It's why we are here. [Connection] is what it's all about." During her research, when Brené asked people about love, they told her about

---

37   Brené Brown, "The Power of Vulnerability," TEDxHouston, June 2010, video 20:04.

heartbreak. When she asked people about belonging, they told her about painful experiences of not fitting in. She said, "Anytime you ask about *connection*, people talk about being *disconnected*."[38]

We talk about disconnection out of shame. According to Brené, shame is "the fear of sharing something about yourself that if other people see it or experience it, you think you won't be worthy of connection." Shame is a universal experience and something that everyone feels. Those that don't experience shame don't experience empathy or human connection. The thing about shame, Brené says, is that "no one wants to talk about it, and the less you talk about it, the more you have it."[39] I was ashamed of failing to jump the curb because I was ashamed of being picked last. As a result, I was ashamed of not being good enough, and I thought that how *good* I was measured my worth.

Because I lacked the belief that I was worthy of belonging, I numbed vulnerability out of fear of being imperfect. Numbness, not toughness, was what I was truly cultivating. My fears of being imperfect in the eyes of my neighbors and myself, made me feel I was unworthy of happiness. To me, *tough* became synonymous with compartmentalizing the hard feelings, which meant being unable to feel the great ones.

---

38 Ibid.
39 Ibid.

THE POWER OF WORDS

My senior year of high school, I was nominated by my classmates as "Best to walk behind" for our Senior Bests. Superlative awards were designed to be fun, lighthearted, and confidence-boosting. The other awards—"Most athletic," "Most likely to be famous," and "Funniest"—indicated that the winner was talented at something. "Best to walk behind" made me feel sexualized, and even worse, I felt like I had to walk into school after everyone or arrive early to class so people wouldn't walk behind me and make comments about my butt. I was nervous about our high school volleyball games because rather than being respected for my athleticism, I knew my peers first looked at my physique in my volleyball spandex. I felt misunderstood, ashamed, and disrespected.

I grew up in an environment where women pay to be fixed in a way that isn't their unique selves, but a version of who they're told they should be. I, too, believed my body needed to be fixed. Brené Brown refers to this as peoples' need to perfect everything, as we can see in popular procedures where surgeons remove fat from someone's waist and inject it somewhere else in their body. My need to fix myself resulted in a seven-year on-and-off struggle with eating disorders and body dysmorphia. Rather than telling myself that I'm "imperfect and wired for struggle, but am worthy of love and belonging," as Brené suggests, I told myself I needed to fit in.[40] I wanted to take what I was blessed with and remove it altogether. If I didn't jump the curb or look the part, I wasn't worthy.

---

40   Ibid.

My inner foundation looked like an 9.0 earthquake had struck four times. The pieces inside of me pulled apart as the gaps between those cracks widened and each of the pieces went in their own toxic direction. I built my foundation on mismatched puzzle pieces from a social construct of how I thought I should be.

I felt like I was living in that claw game at the arcade, trying to grab a stuffed toy I thought would bring me happiness. Everyone knows it's nearly impossible to snag a toy, and if you do, you have to settle for the one that's easiest to get. I spent incredible amounts of time, money, and energy yearning after a life I didn't want and that I knew would never make me feel whole.

My culture and my mind kept making me play this silly game. Any time I lost this impossible game, I hit myself with those words I wouldn't say to my worst enemy: *"You're dumb, you're chubby, and you're just not good enough."* I launched myself into a downward spiral of shame, taking it out on my appearance. I would head to the store to buy comfort food that would make me feel even more guilty and then to the toilet to forget anything had ever happened. I compartmentalized the pain of making myself sick until I felt numb, then told myself, *"Be tough."* I knew I was hurting myself, but the idea of not being who I was conditioned to be outweighed the pain I caused myself.

Eating disorders conquered my world and became my life-threatening reality, but I often didn't *look* like I had one. While they're prevalent among a large amount of people, they don't look the same for everyone. One-third of Division 1 college athletes have reported experiencing an eating disorder. Thirty million Americans—20 million women and 10 million men—reported having an eating disorder in their lifetime.[41] I never reported mine, and I know many other athletes who didn't either. How could we when we were just trying to *be tough*? I became an expert on hiding my shame and guilt and used everything from overt optimism to cleaning supplies to cover my tracks.

My eyes would tell people, "I need help," but my lips didn't follow. Instead, I smiled and pretended. How can you admit vulnerability when you're taught your worth is tied to a toy in a claw machine you'll never get?

I'll never forget when my mom found me after my first semester of college, cleaning up my toilet and thirty pounds lighter. While I don't know what it's like to find your daughter like that, I imagine it's horrific.

I know my mom felt like and still feels like she failed me. I know she was scared and worried out of her mind. I know she wanted to hold me and tell me everything was going to be okay even though she had no idea what to do. I know she knew that I'm stubborn as hell and that I'd resist her help in every way. It's not her fault, and it never was her fault. I need her to know that. I didn't get help, but I tried as hard as I could to do it my own way. After all, I'm a fixer. At least that's what I was telling myself when, really, I was trying my best to be someone else's description of perfect. *Be tough.*

---

41 Vanessa Caceres, "Eating Disorder Statistics," *US News*, February 14, 2020.

I thought success would change everything. As it turned out, though, being named an All-American in your sport after overcoming two knee surgeries and leading one of the most successful women's collegiate soccer programs didn't make the feeling of unworthiness go away. I had cleared the curb, but my worth was still tied up in whether or not I could clear the next one, rather than being born worthy of making the jump.

As soon as my success was over and as soon as I didn't have my teammates to focus on, I rescinded back into a dark hole where my thoughts were angry, nasty, and completely destructive. I learned that distracting myself with external voids will never make internal struggles dissipate. I never fully healed my wounds; I just slapped a *toughness* label on them.

REDEFINING TOUGH

I remember one day, two years after I graduated, I was on a run, deeply entranced in thoughts about my deepest pains: my reconstructive knee surgeries and my eating disorder. Tears welled up in my eyes as Kesha's song "Praying" started softly playing through my headphones. I couldn't remember what it felt like to blow out both of my knees or to feel emotion in a romantic relationship. I cried because I couldn't feel. I had compartmentalized all of the parts that hurt the most and hid behind fake happiness, always smiling, no matter what.

A friend told me that when she feels depressive episodes, "I just sit and let myself feel it." With these words in mind, I've started a journey to feel—not to shy away from or control—just to feel. And in this process of feeling, I ask myself, *"How am I talking to myself right now? What would I say to my friend if she was saying this about herself?"*

I worked so hard to make my issues with mental health disappear, as if they were a cold treatable with antibiotics. But looking back, I know that I never healed from this sickness, and I never will. That's the thing with mental health I'm learning to accept—I don't think it ever *heals*. What I do know is that it begins with the way I talk to myself, the words with which I fuel myself, and the foundation on which I stand. Healing means carefully and lovingly gluing my cracks back together while making sure those pieces are part of who I am, not a puzzle piece designed for someone else.

I still have my internal earthquakes, but I've learned to sit with those thoughts. I feel them. I'm being vulnerable with myself because I know I'm worthy. Period.

My motto used to be "Leave everybody better than you found them," but this can only work if you include yourself. You have to put the oxygen mask on yourself first. Now, my motto is "Leave everybody better than you found them. This includes yourself, every day." After all, we have to fight our inner monsters before we can choose to fight for others. The journey of loving ourselves lasts forever, and it's undeniably my life's greatest battle. But, if I've learned anything from sports, it's that the greatest battles are the ones most worth training, sacrificing, and fighting for.

Brené says there are three ways in which someone striving for wholeheartedness can feel worthy:

First, you must let yourself be profoundly and vulnerably seen.[42] For me, this means allowing myself the worthiness to be loved and accepting someone else's love even though it may look and feel different than what I had planned.

Second, you must practice gratitude and joy in moments of fear and terror, saying, "I'm grateful because to feel vulnerability is to be alive."

Third—and according Brené, the most important—is "You must *believe* that you are enough."[43]

The first thing the orthopedic surgeon says you must do after having knee reconstruction is to straighten your knee. Straightening your knee is the start to gaining back full mobility and giving you a better chance of becoming a great athlete again. It sounds easy, but its simplicity, redundancy, and dull pain makes it extremely uncomfortable. Straightening my knee became my new tough—the opposite of numb. It means feeling the simple things like having a light-hearted conversation with a friend. It means feeling the redundant, like practicing self-love even when I want to do anything but. It means feeling the pain of darkness as much as I feel the joy of light. It means feeling the resilience of never stopping and having faith that I'll make it.

My biggest fear to this day is wasting my life. I think this fear started because I knew I was sick, and I stayed sick for

---

42 Brené Brown, "The Power of Vulnerability," TEDxHouston, June 2010, video 20:04.

43 Ibid.

so long. I'm here to tell you that if you have struggled to believe your worth like I have, you haven't wasted any part of your life. You're living the best you know how. Don't give up and continue to practice cherishing yourself as often as you can every day.

When you truly believe that you're worthy, you'll feel it. You'll get a warm, tingling sensation in your chest that stretches to your fingertips and your toes. That feeling is your magic; it's your superpower energy warming up and preparing to ignite. Believe in your worth, because what you can do with it is almost superhuman.

As we embark on this journey of vulnerability together, identify the moments where you feel like you can't be fully seen.

1. Ask yourself, *"Why don't I feel seen or why won't I allow myself to feel fully seen?"* Write all of your answers down.

_____

2. Then ask yourself, relating to these moments of vulnerability, *"What am I most grateful for?"*

_____

3. Lastly, commit to taking action and to not shy away from any feeling. Instead, embrace them all. *"What will my first action step be?"*

_____

CHAPTER 7

GET BACK UP

———

To me, bliss feels like diving under a wave in the ocean. The energy of the salty, refreshing water pulls my hair back and pushes my lower body forward. All I can hear is the distant and muted energy of the wave—electrifying yet peaceful. As the wave curls and crashes, my body catapults above water. I arise from the water feeling powerful and the Earth seems still. The sun glistens off the top of the water and my face embraces the warmth. Immersed in the energy of a wave, for that moment, all I think about is the exhilaration of feeling connected with the ocean's physicality and the liberation to just feel. It's my ultimate paradise.

Resilience is like diving into a 51-degree wave in the Pacific Ocean in the middle of winter. The first wave you dive under freezes your lungs and you come up for air unable to breathe. The second wave comes just as you're finally able to exhale but now your limbs are numb and shivers spread from your spine to all of your extremities. The third wave comes with more force than the other two waves. You're finally used to the numbness but you're not quick enough to dive under before the wave breaks. Your feet tangle in the whitewash, and you tumble like laundry. Your limbs feel like overcooked pasta as you try to get your head above water. Salt water enters your nose and tingles your brain. The freezing temperature of the water is now your second concern after surviving the relentless whitewash and repeated pounding of waves.

Fear strikes and you panic, wondering if this is the end. But you finally surface and are able to breathe. You made it—at least for the few seconds before the next wave comes. With each passing wave, you get a little warmer, a little faster to beat the crash, and a little more resilient.

Resilience is the act of recovering or adjusting when you experience change or a setback.[44] Resilience presents itself in many different ways during our individual journeys to freedom and excellence. For some, resilience looks like sprinting across a finish line in a workout despite your mind and body wanting to quit or staying up late to re-write a paper multiple times. For others, it's fighting to put food on the table, surviving through battles with mental health, or persevering when life and people intentionally throw you into pounding waves that are nearly impossible to survive. Either way, the resilience we build in the little moments—like getting out of bed when all you want to do is hide under the covers—gives us stamina for the moments that require our utmost strength, whether internal or physical.

---

44 "Resilience (adj.)," *Merriam-Webster*, s.v., accessed January 21, 2021.

"You may not control all the events that happen to you, but you can decide not to be reduced by them."[45]

MAYA ANGELOU

Small acts of resilience push us toward the freedom we feel when diving under a wave; we don't feel like we're suffocating but *thriving*; we don't feel numb but *powerful*.

BALANCE BEAMS

A balance beam is a piece of wood four inches wide, roughly four feet off the ground, and sixteen feet long.[46] It demands tremendous grace on a surface so small you can wrap your fingers around nearly three of its sides. The body of a balance beam is clothed in leather for a small amount of grip and cushion when gymnasts launch their bodies in the air, forced to orient their bodyweight and land perfectly straight. The balance beam requires the utmost strength, balance, and flexibility, as it amplifies even the slightest twitch. It demands *balance*, but it stands for unwavering *resilience*.

We see women gymnasts perform out-of-body performances on the balance beam with tremendous grace and beauty, rarely falling. When a gymnast even wobbles on the beam, we gasp as if she has done something terrible. We remark at gymnasts' ability to execute perfection on a tiny surface designed to test their excellence and resilience to the greatest

---

45 Peggy Anderson, "Great Quotes from Great Women," Simple Truths, Imprint of Sourcebooks, Inc., Illinois, book, p. 17, 2017.

46 "Balance beam," *Encyclopedia Britannica*, accessed January 21, 2021.

degree. What we don't see are the hours of daily practice on the balance beam, from learning a skill to mastering it in order to score a perfect ten.

Most people consider the balance beam to be one of the most difficult of the four apparatuses on which female gymnasts perform, yet it was Jordyn Wieber's—the 2011 World Gymnastics Champion and the 2012 Olympic Gymnastics Gold Medalist—strongest event.[47] Since capturing the world's attention as a gymnastics prodigy in 2011, Jordyn has remained one of the most influential voices in gymnastics and continues to trailblaze and reimagine the future of the gymnastics world today.

Jordyn was a pivotal member of the "Fierce Five" in the 2012 London Olympics along with Gabby Douglas, McKayla Maroney, Aly Raisman, and Kyla Ross. "Fierce Five" was the name they came up with in the Athlete's Village, moments before the 2012 Olympic Opening Ceremony. They debated over names such as the "Fab Five," "Fantastic Five," "Friendly Five," and "Fearsome Five," but "Fierce Five" stuck and ended up symbolizing so much more than an Olympic Gold Medal; it represented a lifetime of resilience of getting back on their feet despite any and every challenge they faced.[48]

In 2019, Jordyn gave a TED Talk at her alma mater, UCLA, about how her relationship with the beam and gymnastics in general helped her accomplish the greatest challenges of her

---

47 Melissa Cruz, "Why Male Gymnasts Don't Do the Balance Beam," *Bustle*, August 11, 2016.

48 "How the Fierce Five Olympic Gymnastics Team got its Nickname," *NBC Sports: Olympic Talk*, April 16, 2020.

life. Jordyn said, "It seems so simple, but in a weird, cumulative way, the nature of gymnastics teaches you resilience. Every day, every time you do a skill and wobble and fall off, you get back up. That right there is resilience."[49]

Jordyn arrived at the 2012 London Olympics as the reigning Gymnastics World Champion and, as a result, most predicted her to win the gold medal in the Individual All-Around competition. Winning the All-Around Competition—being the best gymnast collectively on every gymnastics apparatus—was something she dreamed about and worked for from the time she first stepped into a gym at four years old until she competed in the Olympics at eighteen years old.

It was the day of the Individual All-Around competition and Jordyn recalled looking up at the scoreboard after she finished competing in all four gymnastics events. She missed qualifying for the Individual All-Around finals by two tenths of a point. 38.7 million people tuned in to watch the gold medal favorite miss out on her dreams for something as little as a slightly bent knee or an un-pointed toe. She recalls, "In that moment, it felt like the end of the world." Her thoughts raced. *Why is this happening to me? I worked as hard as I possibly could. Why is it turning out this way?*

---

49   Jordyn Wieber, "How One Olympian Turned Devastation into Inspiration," TEDxUCLA, July 16, 2019, video, 11:07.

"Not qualifying for finals was the lowest point of my life."[50]

JORDYN WIEBER

Two days later, Jordyn had to compete again, this time in the Team All-Around Final Competition. The Team All-Around Final Competition had the same structure as the Individual All-Around in that the total scores from each gymnastics event would be calculated, only this time, the Fierce Five competed collectively for Team USA. The same resilience she practiced since she was four years old helped her pick herself back up in her hotel room and channel her energy and emotions into performing her best on the balance beam in the Team All-Around. Just forty-eight hours after her devastating loss, Jordyn and the Fierce Five won the Team All-Around gold medal.

"That moment of winning a Gold Medal with Team USA became unequivocally the best moment of my life."[51]

JORDYN WIEBER

DAILY ACTS OF RESILIENCE
During my interview with Miss Val, the UCLA Gymnastics head coach and Jordyn's boss while she was an Assistant Coach at UCLA, she told me, "You're not going to be a very

---

50 Ibid.
51 Ibid.

successful athlete if you cannot learn from losing, pick your head up, and try your best next time."

Every time we wobble or fall in life, we can tap back into those daily moments of resilience and learn what we did wrong, how we can improve for next time, and—most importantly—that we can get back up. In moments like the Olympics, you might work for your entire life only to get one or two chances. Jordyn spent fourteen years working for her two chances, and she lost one of them due to an error so insignificant it's hard to fathom. But she took what she had practiced and *chose* to get back on the beam, living out her second and final chance to win Gold. Her daily acts of resilience helped her to lead her team to one of the most prestigious achievements in sports.

When I talked to Jordyn, she told me every time we fall, we have two options: "We can quit, or we can tighten our pony tails a little bit tighter and get back up." The thing about resilience is that when we learn how to get back up on our balance beams, we condition ourselves to be resilient in every area of our lives. We teach ourselves to choose a different outcome than the misfortune forced upon us because we choose to get back up any time a wave knocks us down.

The resilience Jordyn found that allowed her to compete her best in the 2012 Team All-Around is what ultimately helped her come to terms with the fact she had been sexually abused as a child. Her resilience is what helped put her and her teammates' perpetrator behind bars.

In 2018, Jordyn read her last testimony in front of the United States Senate. It was the seventh time she did this, courageously recounting her story of being sexually assaulted by USA Gymnastics Team doctor, Larry Nassar, who was convicted of molesting over five hundred female children and women during his tenure. Jordyn's Fierce Five teammates were also among some of these minors.

Jordyn told me Larry treated all of her injuries from ages eight to eighteen. He earned her trust, always acting as the good guy by bringing Jordyn and her teammates food and coffee when they feared eating in front of their coaches who created an "intense and restricting" environment. His training room served as the athletes' safe place. Jordyn said, "I didn't know these were all grooming techniques he used to manipulate me and brainwash me into trusting him." When Jordyn was fourteen years old, she suffered a hamstring injury, and Larry's medical treatment was a disguise to sexually abuse Jordyn.

All the world and USA Gymnastics cared about was how well the gymnasts performed and that these gymnasts executed their routines flawlessly. Jordyn said, "Nobody was protecting us from being taken advantage of. Nobody was concerned whether or not we were being sexually abused." It took Jordyn sixteen months and six days to go from what she referred to as "denial to acceptance" that she was a victim of child abuse.[52]

---

52 Ibid.

"I am a victim, but I will not live my life as one."

JORDYN WIEBER

Even to this day, outsiders still ask Jordyn, "How did you not know when you were fourteen or even sixteen? How did you not know that was sexual abuse?" She told me, "They don't know what they're doing to me and to all the other victims of Larry Nassar when they say that—when they victim blame."

She recognized that she had control over whether or not she lived as a victim and how she would heal from the abuse she had experienced. She knew this because of the countless times she tightened her ponytail and jumped back on the beam, despite how imperfect the judges said her performance was or how many times she fell. A score never dictated her choice to jump back on; instead she chose to keep moving forward.

There's no right way or answer for how we can get through difficult circumstances; there was no right way for Jordyn to win at the most prestigious level in sports or for her to correctly deal with being a victim. There's only the choice to continuously stand up, jump back on the balance beam, and pursue the outcome you set for yourself.

"It's not necessarily what happens. It's what you do afterward that really matters."[53]

JORDYN WIEBER

In 2019, Jordyn Wieber became the head coach of the University of Arkansas Women's Gymnastics team, making her the youngest-ever NCAA head coach at the age of twenty-three. Prior to this, and immediately after her Olympic and professional career, Jordyn worked as the volunteer assistant gymnastics coach at UCLA under Miss Val while attending UCLA as a student. To this day, Jordyn models the resilience that gymnastics taught her. "I not only personally deal with tough stuff every single day, but I also coach a team of athletes and try to help them understand how important it is to get back up and keep moving after you experience a failure or a setback."

Jordyn describes the score of ten for which all gymnasts aim as "the illusion of perfection. Gymnastics is how well you can do your routine to the judges' ideas of what perfect is, from the time you raise both hands and smile at the judges to when you close your routine the same way." She says, "There's no such thing as perfection." The quest for perfection isn't realistic, rather, it's the culmination of the daily acts of resilience we perform that allows us to be able to execute something excellently.

---

53 Wieber, "How One Olympian Turned Devastation into Inspiration," TEDxUCLA.

By pure statistics alone, Jordyn Wieber has already become one of the most successful women ever, and not just in her age group. She isn't just a great athlete. She isn't just a survivor. She isn't just a public speaker. She isn't just a leader. She can't be singularly defined by a characteristic but by the union of them all coupled with her unique sense of style, ambition, and personality. She's a woman who exudes passion, humility, joy, infectious energy, gratitude, and grit. Her resilience and her relentlessness to choose how she responds to failure are just two of her superpowers.

MORNING RUNS

When we make the decision to not be reduced to what has happened to us, we show our resilient attitude. Jordyn Wieber showed us resilience in attitude by choosing positive ways to respond to terrible situations and grabbing hold of the outcomes she wanted to happen. How we react and the method through which we react is a reflection of our values. These daily acts test not only our overall resilience but also our resilience in our values—how closely we'll stay true to who we are despite everything that tests us.

Anne Mahlum, the founder and CEO of [solidcore], personifies resiliency in her values. [solidcore] is a full body workout that combines intense Pilates and strength training using proprietary machines. The boutique fitness company started in Washington, DC, in 2013 and has since expanded to over seventy studios across more than twenty states in 2021. Prior to [solidcore], Anne founded Back on My Feet, a nonprofit company designed to help homeless people through running which now has a chapter in fourteen major cities. Its members have run a combined 1.2 million miles and have earned over seven thousand jobs and homes. Back on My Feet has also provided over three thousand educations and trainings in just seven years.[54]

Anne started two companies in two completely different industries, yet the goals of these companies are the same: build resilient communities through sport and teamwork. Anne's loyalty and love for her teams permeates in ways that resonate deeply with me as someone who grew up in the sports community. I know the strength and camaraderie you can build, especially when, like Anne, you develop a team whose purpose is rooted in helping people champion their lives and winning together.

When Anne headed out on her daily 6:00 a.m. run, she would always run past the same three homeless men who stood on a corner near her home. They would cheer her on as ran, and she would wave and say hello back. A friendship between them formed, and she looked forward to seeing them as she embarked on her run every morning. Back on My Feet started with on simple question: "How can I get these guys to run with me?"

She knew how impactful running was in her life and how powerful it could be for these men, too. When I interviewed Anne, she told me, "I could tell that they wanted a better life for themselves and they were willing to work for something bigger than what they had right then." She realized she not only wanted to talk to them, but she also wanted to run with

---

54 "Impact," Back On My Feet, 2021.

them. Anne decided to contact the local homeless shelter about formalizing a running club. Anne would provide the shoes if the shelter would allow the men to run with her three days a week.

These homeless men needed sustainable, basic physiological and safety needs like food, water, housing, and a job. But before that could become a reality, Anne knew they had to first build their self-confidence and prove to themselves they were dedicated to rebuilding their lives. Anne told me, "If you met somebody, regardless of whether they were homeless or not, and they told you they run three days a week at 6:00 a.m., you'd think they were disciplined, ambitious, dependable, and respectable. They're someone you'd probably want to have on your team."

Running and committing to something multiple times a week altered the identity of these homeless men and women. Their resilience also changed many outsiders' negative connotations associated with homelessness and showed them that homeless people had the ability to create a better life for themselves.

Anne leveraged her public relations and marketing background to garner the interests of the press and community at large to scale Back on My Feet nationwide. Within a couple of years, Back on My Feet became one of the fastest growing nonprofits in the country and within five years was deeply rooted in fourteen cities.

Six years after starting Back on My Feet, Anne took a step back and looked at the path ahead of her. Her sweet spots were creating, executing, building, and scaling the beginning stages of a company, but she knew that Back on My Feet needed to grow deeper into the communities it was already in rather than expand to new places. Knowing she had given Back on My Feet all she had and that the nonprofit needed experts who were better suited for deep-rooted community growth, she decided to transition into a new venture.

While on the pursuit to build her next company, Anne was still an avid athlete and decided to take her first Pilates class. For twelve years of Anne's life, she had struggled with body image and bulimia. She worked out as much as she could during the day and ate foods with high protein, no fat, and no carbs in order to consume the minimum number of calories possible. She found herself lying to family and friends about why she couldn't go to dinners or holiday celebrations as a cover up for how poorly she thought about the way she looked. This all-consuming body shaming took up so much of her mental and physical energy when all she wanted was to just feel good. She came out of her first Pilates class after getting her "butt kicked" by the workout and realized how tremendous the effect of a low-impact, slow movement class had on her both mentally and physically. She soon became an avid Pilates athlete which helped her transform the way she thought about her body.[55]

Anne knew she could emulate the sports and teamwork-oriented community she built at Back on My Feet in a Pilates-focused environment that would impact a new audience. With

---

55 Rebecca Minkoff, "Anne Mahlum Gets to the Core of the Matter," in *Superhero Women*, produced by Rebecca Minkoff, November 2019, podcast, 28:20.

zero experience in the fitness industry but a passion for sharing the mental and physical strength Pilates had brought her, Anne opened her first [solidcore] studio in Washington, DC, in November 2013. Anne focused on community building to ensure that people had an amazing experience when they entered the studio, knowing the workout would sell itself. Anne told me she continuously focuses on three audiences:

"My employees, my clients, and my investors. Whenever I make decisions, I think about those three groups and make sure I'm acting in the best interest of them."

ANNE MAHLUM

She said, "I wanted people to feel seen, supported, and challenged. Clients kept coming back to [solidcore] because of those two things: the incredible workout and the way that the [solidcore] community made them feel. This was the foundation of our growth." It was a similar foundation to the one Anne had so successfully built with Back on My Feet—taking people on a journey of resilience and helping prove their worth to themselves, no matter the conquest.

COMMITMENTS
Anne's resilience in her values and commitments to herself, her team, and her community remain at the center of her leadership. When I asked Anne about how she exemplifies resilience in her company, she responded that she chooses to "think about it like being on a sports team. We stand up

for ourselves. We have political values as a company and I do as a person. That can permeate into our brand."

On February 23, 2020, a Black man named Ahmaud Arbery was murdered by two armed white men while he was on a jog in a South Georgia neighborhood. It took four months of political pressure from social activist groups for officials to officially arrest these white men who were caught on camera gunning down Ahmaud.[56]

Anne took a public stand on Ahmaud's murder, decrying the horrific details of his death and the racism that infiltrates America. [solidcore] received several emails from clients, saying they were canceling their membership because Anne was being too political. Anne responded to these clients telling them they had the right to do what they wanted with their membership. She told me, "You will never hear me say that our values and principles are for everybody, and we're not saying that anyone else's are wrong."

Anne concluded our interview by saying, "At [solidcore], we let you know where we stand when the going gets tough, and we will not shy away or not be vocal about what we believe is right. We're not just about turning a profit. We're about building a foundational brand." As soon as Anne took an investment in 2017, she set aside some of her personal equity for her [solidcore] employees to own based off of their role and tenure at the company. She said, "I can't say that I'm liberal and only create wealth for the top 0.5 percent of

---

56 Richard Fausset, "What We Know About the Shooting Death of Ahmaud Arbery," *The New York Times*, December 17, 2020.

[solidcore]," which would be Anne and her investors. She recognized her team on the ground was contributing daily to [solidcore]'s success and she understood the importance of giving them the opportunity to earn compounding wealth as a result.

I learned from both Jordyn, Anne, and the Back on My Feet members that resilience should be in every value we uphold and in every action to which we commit. If we make the commitment to show up to a game after missing out on our individual dream, then we show up to the game for our teammates. If we make the commitment to run three days a week at 6:00 a.m., then we take action to wake up, tie our shoes, and get moving. If we make the commitment to accept a job, then we take actions to prepare ourselves for that job. If we make the commitment to stand up for racial justice, then we take action to speak out when we see racism and hold steadfast. *If we make a commitment to be a teammate, then we take action to support our teammates when they're in need.*

Our many commitments vary in size and depth. For some of us, our commitments are in the pursuit of lifelong goals— maybe a promotion or a dream job, like Jordyn becoming an Olympian and a head coach. For others, commitments might be to accept things we cannot control and to honor and love ourselves for surviving and getting through.

Before we can make commitments to others, we need to make commitments of resilience to ourselves. Anne said, "If you care too much about what people think, you're just not going to make it as a CEO. The criticism will drown you." Most of resilience is believing in yourself when no one else will.

When we truly believe our worth—that deep-seated feeling of choosing yourself, your joy, and your passions—we find it within ourselves to do our little acts of resilience every day, no matter what freezing wave approaches us.

Be resolute in your attitude and focus on your values. Continue jumping back on the balance beam and keep standing up for what holds true to you, your values, and your team. Your resilience will take you from hardship to greatness.

CHAPTER 8

BECOME THE LEADER
OF YOUR OWN LIFE

SUMMER FITNESS PACKET

Every summer in college, we were given the Summer Training Packet—a packet designed to prepare our fitness for the upcoming pre-season when we reported back to campus in early August. It felt like soccer summer school. Most of us didn't grow up near one another, so our only accountability was through texts, calls, or FaceTimes. We went from the extreme structure of having strength and soccer coaches telling us what to do every day and a team to battle through workouts with during the schoolyear to being completely on our own during the summer. We only had ourselves to cross the finish line. There were no teammates to shove us across if we weren't going to make it.

Many of our teammates had summer internships at big banks, hospitals, consulting firms, and start-ups, so our only opportunity to train was well before the sun came up or after it went down. We were accustomed to juggling multiple high-pressure responsibilities, but summers were the first time we had to take ownership of the type of player we were going to be when we came back to campus.

Our coach used to tell us before we left that our commitment over the summer—our physical and mental preparation—set the precedent for the rest of the next season, and he was right. Our physical stamina was really a test of our mental muscles.

How far was I willing to go mentally for training, recovery, and discipline so that I could follow physically?

What were the habits I was building and were those sustainable through a season?

How was I preparing to be the best teammate and leader possible to ensure I wasn't letting my teammates down?

Was my preparation setting us up to become Big East Champions?

These summers tested my willpower, my grit, my discipline, my servitude, and my champion mindset. The Summer Fitness Packet symbolized the actions we'd take to get raw and real with ourselves and understand what makes us, us. On the twenty-fourth 100-yard sprint by ourselves, how do we keep going when all we feel is pain?

Before I started to take action on being a Superhero to others, I needed to build my inner Superhero and take the lead in my own life. I awakened my inner Superhero by first discovering the unique values that keep me grounded. Here are some values I've learned from the women I interviewed and came across. These values are strategically in this order, because for me, I've learned I can't fully achieve one value without the others that precede it.

BE TRUE TO YOUR CHILD SELF

Glennon Doyle, activist and author of three *New York Times* Bestsellers, *Untamed, Love Warrior,* and *Carry On, Warrior,* taught me to be true to my child self—the girl I was before I was told who I was supposed to be. In her book *Untamed,* Glennon describes how her then-girlfriend, Abby Wambach, one of the greatest American soccer players, asked Glennon's parents for her hand in marriage. Glennon's mom choked on her tears of joy and responded, "Abby, I have not seen my daughter this alive since she was ten years old."[57]

Glennon was forty years old and had been married to a man for twelve years, with whom she had three children, before she fell in love with and later married Abby. *Untamed* documents her process of unscrewing the bolts of the cage in which she felt she was locked, intentionally and voraciously removing all of the bars to find herself and to re-construct her entire life's framework.[58]

Based on psychological and environmental studies, Glennon found that age ten is when young boys and girls start to learn where and how they fit into societal norms. She wrote, "I wanted to be a good girl, so I tried to control myself. I chose

---

57   Glennon Doyle, *Untamed,* (New York: The Dial Press, 2020), 352.
58   David Kenyon, "The Best Soccer Players in United States Women's National Team History," *Bleacher Report,* June 4, 2019.

a personality, a body, a faith, and a sexuality so tiny I had to hold my breath to fit myself inside. Then I promptly became very sick … all of the things that make a woman human are a good girl's dirty secret."[59] The process of trying to fit in a tiny cage suffocated her. Her counter-process—her exhale—translated into an eating disorder and drug and alcohol abuse. Glennon wrote, "None of us can hold our breath all the time … I understand myself differently now. I was just a caged girl made for wide-open skies. I wasn't crazy. I was a goddamn cheetah."

This chapter, "Sparks," makes me think about how my destructive self-talk led me down a dark path of reducing myself. As Glennon describes, it was the one way I felt like I could fit inside of my cage. I had to find myself again. But in order to find myself, I had to remember myself. I took myself back to my elementary school and to my favorite after-school program, Cartoon Art. We literally sat in the classroom learning how to draw cartoons in any way we could imagine. The class would sometimes end early, so our teacher let us escape to the playground before the school bus drove us home.

At the time, I was in third grade. My teacher, Mrs. Lemon, rewarded us with Lemonhead candies when we did something well. Plus, she had just seated me next to my new best friend, Hannah. My favorite things were learning cursive and having competitions on the monkey bars.

---

59 Doyle, *Untamed*, 5.

One day after Cartoon Art class, wearing a white and blue dress with a Strawberry Go-Gurt stain on the left side, I skipped and stumbled down to the playground with my classmate Ryan, carelessly wandering in naive delight. We climbed monkey bar after monkey bar, seeing who could make it across the fastest and run backward up the slide first. We did the circuit until the teacher forced us to stop. When the teacher wasn't watching, I snuck in a few flips around the monkey bars, my right leg hooked around the six-inch-thick yellow bar. Whoever had the "puffiest" blisters on their plum-sized palms automatically won first place. We were exhausted after fifteen minutes but desperately wanted to play longer. My memory ends with our teacher blowing her whistle and summoning us to the bus line.

This moment wasn't my last memory of being uncaged, but it remains a fond example of what it meant to be myself and to play unbothered. I was more bummed about not being able to eat the Strawberry Go-Gurt that had fallen on my dress than the fact that I had ruined a pretty dress. Before I knew what perfect looked like, I just knew what I loved and what made me happy. I had no idea what my cage would look like, let alone that I was destined for one.

When I think of this moment, I'm reminded of the fact that I love to play. Playing brings me euphoria. Playing is my love language because it's what made me love myself. Before I was ten, loving myself was my instinct—something I felt in my gut—but it wasn't intentional. I just didn't know otherwise. Now, loving myself has to be intentional, because after being caged, not loving myself became my learned instinct.

I also had to be honest with myself about the things that made me unhappy as much as the things that made me happy. Exhaling and purging my worries in the form of bulimia actually made me happy. It took me awhile to admit that fact but purging momentarily dissipated my worries. For that hour, I could be free if my friends or family didn't catch me hurting myself. Seven years of destruction later, as I unscrewed the bolts and removed the steel bars from my cage, I knew I needed to identify what was causing me to hold my breath. I needed to find an exhale that wasn't harmful and that didn't reduce me, and I needed to build armor against the things that did.

Unloving myself meant punishing myself for being who I wasn't rather than embracing myself for being who I was. I unlearned how to *un-love* and learned how to *love* by documenting everything in my composition notebook and by going to therapy. I defined four pillars for myself that I had to achieve daily in order to be happy. Those pillars were physical, mental, spiritual, and emotional. I wanted to play, to learn or discuss something that stimulated my thoughts and strengthened my brainpower, to re-discover my faith in a way that supported human rights, not pro-hibited them, and to experience deep connections with people and take a true chance at love, unafraid of being heartbroken.

With these four pillars, I built a bridge to finding myself again and left the cage I wasn't fit to live in. I wanted to be my energetic and feisty third grade self with a Go-Gurt-stained dress and oozing blisters. Therapy—in the form of a clinical therapist, physical exercise, and being open with friends and peers about my struggles—has guided my path to re-discovering myself and reimagining a life I know I deserve.

On this journey toward finding my true self by looking back on who I was as a child, I learned that the idea of just wanting to be normal had become synonymous with the coveted idea of authenticity flashing on all of our devices as every brand's new ad campaign. To be authentic, I felt I had to conform to some sort of standard set by those who are in charge. Authenticity, to me, became toxic comparison. When we normalize something raw and real like eating disorders, we make open dialogue about eating disorders okay and on the same playing field as talking about nutrition. This is helpful. But when we normalize false authenticity like an edited magazine cover photo that we categorize as real, we're telling people how they should be. We're taking what makes each individual beautiful and locking them into cages, making them feel as if their true selves aren't good enough. This is a destructive, societal dilemma, but it's one that can be solved at the individual level.

First, we must find our childhood selves and commit them to memory. When we recall the purest forms of our beings, we can begin to break free of our cages, build a bridge out of our pillars, and skip (or even stumble) to our freedom.

BE KIND AND TREAT PEOPLE WITH RESPECT

It was the first day of my internship at Edelman, one the largest global communications firms in the world. My boss, a Senior Account Executive, told me to meet in the ten-seat conference room at 2:00 p.m. sharp. I left our intern open office space in the back-left corner at 1:40 p.m. to walk to the all-glass meeting room just two minutes down the hall, sure I would somehow be late. I was on the Business Development team comprised of senior leaders and myself, the intern.

Kate, my boss's boss, was the Senior Vice President, and I had already heard whispers about her in our intern room. She carried a confident presence, had an energetic ambiance, and was the leader all the interns wanted to get to know. When the meeting started, my boss motioned for me to sit next to her in the seat diagonally across from Kate at the half-filled rectangular table. My boss introduced me to start off the meeting.

Kate smiled at me and said, "Marina, it's so nice to meet you. Don't be afraid to ask questions or speak up. You're a part of this team now." I swallowed, but my anxiously watering mouth sent my saliva down my trachea, forcing me to choke and making my eyes water. I responded, "(cough)-ank you. I'm excited to learn."

Three weeks later, when I finally felt like I was in stride with my role, news broke that Kate was leaving the company. "*This is my only chance*," I thought. I had to get fifteen minutes on her calendar. She was the first woman in a business professional environment to whom I looked up to, mostly because of the way she commanded a room's attention while simultaneously giving everyone the opportunity to feel like part of the team. I asked my boss if I could put time on Kate's calendar, and once she told me I could, I sent Kate a calendar invite for a fifteen-minute meeting. Right after sending the invite, I knew I should've requested just ten minutes instead. *"What was I thinking? Kate didn't have time for me!"*

Kate responded by requesting a change in time. *"I knew it,"* I said to myself.

But I was wrong; Kate had requested the meeting be for forty-five minutes. I yelped out of excitement, getting eye rolls from the other interns that told me to chill out. The day of the meeting, I cruised by her office ten minutes before our meeting, staying on the opposite side of the hallway so she didn't notice me. One long lap later, I arrived at her office seven minutes ahead of schedule. Kate glanced at her watch to see if she was running late. "I'm early, don't worry," I mouthed.

She opened the door right away, smiled, and said, "Come in, Marina. I'm excited to chat!" Immediately, she started talking about her day, filling me in on her move and answering my questions about her career at Edelman. She asked me about my aspirations, what I wanted out of this internship, and told me how I could succeed. As we were coming up on time, I said, "I have one last question. Out of everything you've learned while working at every job in your life, what's the one thing you know to be true and that you practice daily?"

She thought for a moment before looking to the right corner of her desk at the photos of her two-year-old and husband along with Pinterest-type office quotes. Then she looked back at me, leaned forward, put her elbows on her desk, clasped her hands together in a fist, and rested her chin gently on the tops of her knuckles.

With a soft look in her eyes, she said, "You never know what someone brings in their bag for lunch every day. You never know what's going on with them. It's my job, not just as a manager, but as a human who shares a space with them, to treat each person with kindness and respect, every single day." She continued, "To be kind and respectful is a *choice*. It's not always easy, but it's the one thing I've found to be of greatest importance as a human being and an effective leader."

Whenever I'm in a new situation or in one that prompts me to judge someone harshly, I remind myself of Kate's words; "You never know what someone's going through. Treat them with compassion and respect." Kate taught me that being a leader isn't about being right and being overly critical of others in a way that undermines them. Being a leader means using your influence to hear, teach, and elevate people through compassion. However, before we can be compassionate toward others, we have to try and be compassionate toward ourselves, every day—even when we aren't feeling our best. Treating ourselves with respect allows us to be unconditionally respectful to the people around us.

BE VULNERABLE AND EMBARRASS YOURSELF

In 2000, Sara Blakely started Spanx, a shapewear company, with $5,000 she had saved from her day-job selling fax machines. Sara quickly became famous for transforming beauty standards and helping women feel beautiful no matter what size they were. Just twelve years after Sara started Spanx, she became one of the first self-made female billionaires, owning 100 percent of her company.

Twenty years later, Spanx now makes over $400 million in annual sales.[60]

Sara Blakely intentionally seeks moments to embarrass herself, like singing in elevators in front of other people, making everyone—including herself—feel extremely awkward and uncomfortable. "If too much time goes that I haven't embarrassed myself, I can sense it in myself and I'm like, 'I've got to do something embarrassing,' because the fear of embarrassment loses its power over me," she said.[61]

When Sara loses her fear of embarrassment, she also loses the fear of messing up. Sara has been practicing her fearlessness and her tenacity since she was a child. Her father used to ask her and her brother once a week at the dinner table, "What did you fail at this week?" If Sara didn't have anything to share, she would be mad at herself because, to her, that meant she didn't try anything new or something she was afraid of. Her father would then follow up by asking, "What's something positive you learned from that failure?" By re-enforcing the habit of trying something new or conquering a fear, Sara became relentless in her pursuit of her passions and the ideas that swarmed inside her head. She credits being comfortable with failure and relentlessly pursuing out of the box ideas as a major reason why Spanx has been able to continuously innovate and grow.

---

60 Nick Wolny, "Spanx Founder Sara Blakely Says This Business Idea Validation Step Can Be A Big Mistake," *Entrepreneur*, November 4, 2020.

61 James Altucher, "What I Learned from Spanx Founder Sara Blakely," *The James Altucher Show*, February 7, 2017, Podcast, Episode #211, 1:24:02, February 7, 2017.

Sara says that the key to getting over the fear of embarrassing yourself and leading a fulfilling life—not to mention leading a tremendously successful company—is not caring what other people think. "Not caring about what other people think doesn't mean I don't care about them," Sara said. Instead, "I unlearn the idea that my identity and happiness is wrapped up in someone else's idea of me." Rather than focusing on someone's idea of us to dictate our identity and actions, Sara reminds us that practicing being uncomfortable and laughing at ourselves makes us fearless to go after our goals. For one of her first advertising campaigns, Sara took pictures of herself in Spanx and used the before-and-after photos as marketing materials and advertisements in highly trafficked areas. At the time, social media didn't exist and seeing people in underwear wasn't a norm. Sara decided to plaster her booty across town to show the functionality of Spanx.

When trying to earn her first big purchase order from a department store, Sara called the buyer at Neiman Marcus—one of the most high-end department chains—dozens of times before nailing down an in-person meeting. After five minutes into the interview with the immaculately dressed, designer head-to-toe Neiman Marcus buyer staring back at Sara's comparably disheveled and off-brand look, Sara saw she was losing the buyer's attention. At the time, Sara's informal, natural, and fun approach was unprecedented when it came to women's undergarments. [62]

---

62 Ibid.

Sara knew she needed the buyer to see the magic of Spanx—how they made an impossible pair of pants, dresses, or skirts look flawless on a woman's body. Sara asked the buyer if she could go to the women's bathroom with her because Sara needed to show her the before-and-after look of Spanx under light-colored pants that magnified every flaw. Uncomfortable with having to go to the bathroom for a pitch, the buyer reluctantly agreed. As soon as the buyer saw the transformation of how Spanx made Sara look, the buyer made a purchase order to test Spanx in seven Neiman Marcus stores. Today, Spanx is sold in over fifty countries, has extended to all types of women's clothing, and even has a men's line.[63]

In 2017, Sara created her personal Instagram account while she was waiting in an airport to board a flight. She wanted people to follow her on Instagram, so she took a video of herself approaching strangers in the airport terminal, asking them if they would follow her on Instagram. "Hi, my name is Sara," she said, "I just joined Instagram today, and I was wondering if you could follow me." People looked back at her like she was out of her mind, their eyes saying, "*This isn't the way following people is supposed to work.*" She walked up to an aisle where people were facing one another and asked the question again. More people laughed, and one person shouted back, "What did you say?" Sara repeated herself and asked if they would follow her on Instagram. No one knew she was Sara Blakely, and that was exactly her intent. Sara didn't start embarrassing herself because she was famous,

---

63   James Altucher, "What I Learned from Spanx Founder Sara Blakely," The James Altucher Show, February 7, 2017, Podcast, Episode #211, 1:24:02.

rather she embarrassed herself because it made her grounded in who she was, which helped her build an empire.[64]

When I intentionally embarrass myself, I forget about the illusion of perfection that I build up in my mind. I know that I set myself up to laugh and have fun rather than be disappointed by not having an outcome go exactly as I projected. Because I no longer have a dark cloud of disappointment hanging over me, I'm able to fundamentally be kind to and respect myself. I can be vulnerable because I know that I'm worthy of respect and I don't fear what others have to say.

Being kind, respectful, vulnerable, and embarrassing myself are my keys to leading my own life, achieving my goals, and experiencing happiness. Whenever I need a redirect or I don't feel like I'm leading my own way, I come back to these values.

CREATE YOUR OWN SUMMER FITNESS PACKET
At the start of every Summer Fitness Packet, we had a page of our goals and team values. I've recreated this page below. Take the time to fill out your values and determine who impacted those values and why. Then, begin to write the ways in which you can practice those values daily. Then, if you're up for it, think of one way in which you can embarrass yourself.

---

64   Sara Blakeley (@SaraBlakely), "One year ago today..." Facebook, video, 0:53.

VALUE 1

List your value.

_____

_____

Why is it important to you?

_____

_____

Which person has impacted this value and why?

_____

_____

In what small way can you practice this value daily?

_____

_____

What is one way in which you can embarrass yourself?

_____

_____

By completing this exercise for as many values as you hold true, you will begin to garner ownership over your own life.

PART 3

INSPIRE THE MAGIC IN OTHERS

CHAPTER 9

BYE FEMALE RIVALRIES, HELLO FEMALE TEAMMATES

"HERE WE GO. LET'S WIN THE BIG EAST!" Heart, Soccer ball, Heart.

Vashti, my teammate on the Georgetown University Women's Soccer team and my Gameday Buddy, wrote this on a blue sticky note in November 2016. I've kept her note in my soccer bag-turned-backpack-turned-purse ever since. I'll keep it in my bag for the rest of my life.

Vashti gave me a special note before every game along with my favorite candy or snack. By the end of our four-month-long season, the inside of my gym locker was decorated with her colorful sticky notes. Me—the team captain and graduate student—and "Vash"—the freshman who gave her soul in every practice and always had a smile on her face—were linked. She was on her first rodeo and I was on my fifth.

She's from New Jersey and I'm from Southern California. She is 5'6" and I am 6'0". She's Black and I'm white. She quit soccer after her freshman year and I stayed with the team for five. The only things that connected us were sports and our sticky notes.

It was lonely being the captain, especially of a team of women who were exceptional both in the classroom and on the field. I never wanted to let them down. Their expectations for themselves and for our team were sky-high—get the highest GPA, score the best internship or job offer, and be one of the top soccer programs in the nation. Vash's sticky notes were silent, confident whispers of "*You got this*" when I often didn't know whether or not I actually did. It's because of Vash that my bedroom wall and office desk are now decorated with post-it notes of inspirational quotes and confidence-boosting messages to myself.

Vash gave me the blue sticky note the morning of the Big East League Semi-Finals, a tournament featuring the top six teams at the end of Big East season. The winner of the Big East Championship received an automatic bid to play in the NCAA Playoffs against other qualifying college programs across the country. We were slated to play DePaul University, a team to which we had lost by three goals earlier in the season—one of our only three losses. That year was the first time Georgetown Women's soccer won the Big East Championship and made it to the NCAA Final Four. Our next and loss was the National Championship Semi-Finals.

I kept that blue sticky note in my soccer bag the rest of the season for good luck because it fed my athlete superstition after we won the Big East Championship. When our season ended, I sat alone in our locker room, cleaning out collectibles from my locker and my soccer bag. I unzipped the technology pocket of my soccer bag and stumbled upon the blue sticky note, picking off the grass that covered the sticky part. I laughed to myself, thinking about the irony of superstition. You put so much work into preparation, yet you bank on a small inanimate object to bring you the fortune you earned. Truth is, that sticky note symbolized the culmination of what Vash's pump-ups meant to me. It's a memory of our team and how fired up we were to play our games despite the odds against us. None of the outside trash talk or condescension mattered because we had each other. That sticky note represented a teammate bond, and it was the token that reminded me of what being a great teammate meant.

At the most basic level, being a good teammate means treating someone with respect and genuinely wanting your teammate to succeed. This is as simple as asking how their day has been when they arrive at practice or having their back when your competition is talking smack. To fully treat a teammate with respect and want them to succeed, we must honor one another's differences, uniqueness, and special talents. Any outsider could clearly state what made Vash and me different. Our differences mattered insofar as we brought our own specialty to the team, and it is *because of* our differences that her sticky notes were so special. She saw me, and her notes reached me on a profound, vulnerable level that I wasn't able to expose, being the most senior player on the team in the position between the coaching staff and my teammates.

As leaders, our greatest power comes from learning to be a good teammate. Being a teammate teaches us *power with*—*power with* your teammates, together—our differences, similarities, weaknesses, and strengths, uplifting every single person. It should never be *power over* our teammates, pushing someone down. It is *with* our teammates we learn that respect, not hate; elevation, not comparison; and unity, not division are our greatest collective strengths to enable our team's success.

SUPERHERO SQUAD

There are revolutionary elements to being a good teammate that can change the trajectory of a team—ones I was grateful to experience. Both times I blew out my knee, teammates carried me off the field and spent the entire day and night with me. I've been physically shoved across the finish line to pass a fitness test. I've been given a pep talk I needed to play the game of my life. It's when those revolutionary elements of unwavering work ethic, selflessness, and compassion are recognized, celebrated, and encouraged that they can lead a team to remarkable success. It wasn't until the last season of my sports career—my graduate "red shirt" season of college soccer—that I truly understood what these revolutionary elements were. They existed, but I didn't know how to *see* them.

We're taught in sports that the starting line-up, the captain of the team, or those who are given the title of "leader" are who we should all look to as an example of how to act and play. At the professional level, starters' impacts are reinforced by larger paychecks, sponsorship deals, and more publicity. If starters are producing, then they're paid. But we are conditioned to believe that impact is solely defined by results—how many points you score or how many points you don't give up.

You won't find what it means to be a good teammate by just looking at results, especially for legacy programs that have been successful year after year. If you want to understand what makes a great teammate—someone who's selfless, undeniably hard working, unconditionally supportive, and holds the rest of the accountable to their goals—look to the bench.

The non-starters or the "practice squad" don't have room for error. If they mess up, the coach will yell at them—that is, if the coach cares enough. If the coach doesn't care, the players will be kicked out of the drill or even practice altogether. These players must bring high energy, focus, and drive to every practice, event, or competition. They may not have the greatest talent on the team, but they show up every day and give everything they have, knowing their investment is to make other players better. They know that despite their investment, they still may only get three minutes of playing time in a ninety-minute game or when their team is up by three goals.

During my last season, I studied my teammates who rarely received the opportunity to play. Their impact on the team—their energy, passion, hard work, commitment to excellence, respect, and love—is how our team found a way to make it to the Final Four and finish our season ranked third in the nation. They pushed us all—particularly the starting squad—to not just be better soccer players, but better versions of ourselves. They valued our team before themselves and cared not just about their individual success but, more importantly, about our team's. To them, collaboration far outweighed any spotlight. They were the Superhero Squad, using the best of their abilities to elevate everyone around them.

My graduate year, this Superhero Squad knew that supporting one another through mistakes and seeking excellence while having fun was the only way they were going to have a fulfilled season and truly enjoy themselves. They showed me what a good teammate looked like both on and off the field. They were the first to laugh at you, but also the first to defend you if anyone else dared to hurt your feelings.

I will never forget the last practice I played on the Superhero Squad. We were scrimmaging one another in preparation for our next game. It was 6:15 p.m. after over two hours of practice. Our coach divided up our pinnies—the Superhero Squad in yellow and the starting squad in blue. Practice had been exceptionally competitive. We had just taken a huge 0-3 loss on our home field to Stanford University and we were all livid. To lose by that of a high margin on our home field was deflating and embarrassing. To athletes, losing is painful, and it never gets less painful. So, you learn how to lose less often.

The frustration we felt over our fresh loss was palpable from the minute we walked back onto the field for practice. All our team wanted to do was see the field again, play well, and win. We started the day with passing drills designed to refine how we receive and deliver a pass. We would pass the ball ten yards, run to the cone, turn around and receive a pass, then pass it ten yards. It was the simplest skill move and the perfect time to release our tension. As we drilled the ball at each other as hard as we could, each pass hit with a greater velocity.

If a passing drill fired us up, our starters versus non-starters scrimmage was definitely going to get heated. After a while, the score was 0-0 and our coach let us know we had ten minutes left. Of course, none of us were leaving that field until someone put the ball in the back of the net—tying wasn't an option. The starting team had possession of the ball and quickly moved it up the field. I was playing Center Back on the Superhero Squad. Our leading goal scorer had the ball and burned me on two moves, setting herself up to slot the ball in the back of the net. Out of nowhere, our other Center Back performed this unbelievable slide tackle, winning the ball and distributing it to an outside forward on our team. She carried the ball up the sideline, crossed the ball from the left side of the field, and our attacking midfielder slotted the ball in the left-hand corner of the goal. The Superhero Squad won. "Alright, that's good," said our coach.

This moment represented the epitome of what the Superhero Squad stood for: all-out effort until the final whistle, channeling the entire team's negative energy from losing into their own confidence and energy to win. A week later, I looked back and told myself to never forget that moment because it was the last practice I spent on the Superhero Squad. They were my sticky note of what it meant to be a great teammate, and I never wanted to forget the impression they forever imprinted on me. I decided to carry forward the Superhero Squad's approach to life and spread this mindset beyond the soccer pitch.

I haven't talked to some of the Superhero Squad in years, and maybe we were never even super close, but being in their presence, even for a brief moment, gives me a warm feeling—an affirmation in myself that someone else sees me for who I am, and I get them, too. I carry Vash's sticky note everywhere I go because I never want to let the way she and the Superhero Squad made me feel—so sure of myself—go. *"HERE WE GO"* has become one of my daily pump-up mantras.

FEMALE RIVALRY

Female rivalry is the antithesis to female teammates. Rivalry is the opposite of pulling someone up. Talking smack behind someone's back is the opposite of writing a confidence-boosting sticky note.

Female teammate-ship has the power to win championships and conquer unparalleled feats. Female rivalry has the power to tear women down and drive them further apart.

"Why did *she* get the job and not me?"

"Well, she's not cute *and* she's fat, so whatever. Good luck."

"What is he *thinking* being with her?"

"I'm better. I deserve it more."

"I can't wait to watch her fail."

Attacks.

Female on female, full out combat.

What is something you have said about another female—either to yourself or to someone else—that you wish you could take back?

I've said all five of those statements and many more. Female rivalry has poisoned most women, so much so against each other, to the point that making these kinds of statements feels like natural instinct. Like teammate-ship, we have to understand where female rivalry comes from.

Why are women so mean to each other?

Best defined, "female rivalry happens when a woman uses her power to keep another woman down, mistreats her, or competes unfairly."[65] In my perception of society, we are born into a world where sexism is engrained into our daily lives from the time we start to differentiate blue from pink. Women more often than not are taught what we can do and what we cannot do. We are taught what we can wear, how we should put on makeup, and what colors we must like. We are given a rulebook to follow as soon as we start to breathe. We've been taught that this rulebook allows us to breathe, yet it's the thing that suffocates us the most.

Women "internalize sexism ... leading us to mistreat, under-estimate, and distance [ourselves] from other women in order to increase [our] power and standing among men."[66] The

---

65   Mikaela Kiner, "It's Time to Break the Cycle of Female Rivalry," *Harvard Business Review*, April 14, 2020.

66   Ibid.

world tells female athletes they are not as strong, not as capable, and not as entertaining to watch play sports. In the working world, women are taught that they have a limited pool of spots available for them, a limited amount of funding to pull from to start companies, and that because of this, they must battle other women for the one seat at the table. "The precept of 'one seat at the table' comes from a belief that diversity is mandated, but not useful."[67] This idea of one seat at the table is predicated on the idea of affirmative action—the belief that society isn't doing enough systemically, so we need to open more opportunities for marginalized people. This solves an immediate problem, but what it doesn't do is address the root cause: *why* women aren't at the table to begin with and how we can systemically begin to change from the bottom up.

This internalization of sexism stems in part from evolutionary psychology; because men can "impregnate women, we associate our value to them and therefore turn on each other in competition for that prize."[68] Evolutionary psychology tells us that in order to survive and protect ourselves from harm, women need to attract the opposite sex. This competition amongst each other has not just persisted since the dawn of time when women were told their only role in this world was to reproduce but mainstream entertainment also glorifies it. Society has been conditioned to believe we like to see women fight, and more often than not, women attack one another's looks in order to feel validated in our own attractiveness.

---

67   Ibid.

68   Grace Back, "Why Do We Continue to Glorify Female Rivalry? Let's Move On," *Marie Claire,* April 8, 2019.

However, when women have the opportunity to decide what they want, women reported they "invite and value *healthy* competition—fighting fairly for a job, project, or promotion."[69] When women aren't pinned against one another and they aren't fighting for the one female-reserved position, they generally want to win fairly.

To change our outside environment, women need to start by changing our insides—our souls. In order to channel women's negative energy toward one another into the advancement of women, we have to unlearn our internalized sexism.

Rather than sending a nasty text about another woman, why don't we write a post-it note that would boost her up?

Instead of wishing her failure, why don't we think of one thing we can do to help her succeed?

When she blows out her knee, why don't we carry her off the field instead of watching her writhe in pain?

When women "champion the women around her ... [there are] more opportunities and increased success for all."[70] When women start covering each other by performing game-saving slide tackles, all women on the team win. Women won't achieve female equality until we fix the rivalries amongst ourselves. Women won't conquer feats that seem impossible until women do away with rivalry between one another and

---

69   Mikaela Kiner, "It's Time to Break the Cycle of Female Rivalry," *Harvard Business Review*, April 14, 2020.

70   Ibid.

reconcile together, as teammates. Superheroism dies with rivalry, but Superheroism thrives with teammate-ship.

SUPERHERO SQUAD ACTIVITY

Get out your own version of a sticky note. Write a note answering the following question: "What is one thing you can do to be a better teammate?"

Go write a positive, uplifting note to a friend or woman in your life and give it to them so they can stick it on their bedroom wall and be encouraged to spread the teammate-ship. *Repeat throughout your entire life.*

CHAPTER 10

THE SISTERHOOD EFFECT

THE GRIP WE SHARE

On July 1, 2019, Yana-Janell received a call we all dread but never expect: "Your friend Kristian has been in an accident. She's unresponsive and has been airlifted to a medical center. They've removed a portion of her skull to reduce brain swelling and bleeding. She's in a coma and we don't know the status right now ..." Kristian's family told her.

Kristian's car was hit by a reckless driver on a freeway. The car hit the passenger side and the airbags in her new Tesla failed to deploy. Medics airlifted Kristian to the nearest ICU and took her husband and son to a pediatric ICU at a separate hospital.

Kristian and Yana-Janell had been best friends since the third grade, when Kristian transferred to the elementary school Yana-Janell attended in Little Rock, Arkansas. Their relationship started like all childhood friendships do—"You like me, I like you, let's be best friends." This friendship morphed into a sisterhood that would see them through the rites of passage of growing up: first kisses, making the softball team, getting their driver's licenses, college, first jobs, first heartbreaks, starting a family, and starting a company.

Kristian studied the history of science and history of medicine at Yale University before earning a Master of Public Health from Yale. She later received her Doctorate in Public Health from Johns Hopkins, where she earned the title "Doctor." Kristian told me her desire to go out into the world and to immediately affect change in her communities is the driving factor for why she decided to study public health.

Kristian Edwards is the CEO and founder of BLK + GRN and a Professor at the George Washington Milken Institute School of Public Health. BLK + GRN is a Black artisan marketplace supported by musicians like Ariana Grande, renowned DJ and Health Entrepreneur Hannah Bronfman, and professional athletes and Olympians like Sydney Leroux.

While working in public health and avidly consuming organic, all-natural beauty products, Kristian read an article from the Environmental Working Group that showed that products marketed to Black women were more toxic than those marketed to white women. Because of this, Kristian started BLK + GRN, an avenue that enables Black entrepreneurs to sell their toxin-free products and creates a destination for the world to connect with products that truly enhanced their lifestyle.

Kristian has led her life with strength and has always fought for others to have more opportunities. When she sees a problem, she asks herself, *"How can I fix this?"* After the accident, she was fighting for her life and needed others to rally around her.

I think of sisterhood like going on an insane water ride. You and your best friend climb into an inner tube and you slowly approach a torturous and intimidating plastic concave structure. You're excited and know it's going to be fun, but you have this knot in the pit of your stomach in case something might go wrong. Just then, your best friend grabs your hand and holds it as tight as she can. You enter this snake-like structure, unable to see what's next, and you both start screaming at the top of your lungs. The water beneath you tries to knock you both off the inner tube, but you're strong as hell and won't let anything move either of you. Halfway through, you're laughing as hard as you can to the point where you need to gasp for more air as plummet into the water. You re-surface after you both plunged into the pool at the bottom of the ride, and your best friend starts laughing at you because you have the biggest wedgie from your bathing suit.

Sisterhood is that grip you share—that strength and whatever it needs to be in that moment—that will never let you go. When the water is literally pulling you under, that grip holds onto you and fights to pull you up. That grip never, ever quits on you, so you never, ever quit on yourself.

Immediately after that fateful phone call, Yana-Janell flew from Houston to Baltimore—an immediate ticket purchase that can only mean the worst. When Yana-Janell arrived at the hospital, she walked into Kristian's room. Yana-Janell described Kristian as "completely swollen, eyes shut, with staples in her head due to the fact that part of her skull was removed." Machines and contraptions delicately tangled around her sister, keeping her alive.

Yana-Janell soaked in the fact that her best friend's life was hanging by a thread, and she knew she needed to stop panicking and take action. She needed to do every little thing she could to keep the grip strong between herself and Kristian. She needed to be present.

Those rites of passage Yana-Janell and Kristian experienced together—the firsts and the layers in between—became the most important things for survival. "I knew the answers to all of her security questions—like the name of her first boyfriend, what her first job was, or the make and model of her first car—when her parents or husband didn't ..." Yana-Janell continued, "Because I knew the answers to these questions, because I lived through these experiences with her, we were able to get into the bank account to keep Kristian's business afloat; we were able to look up Kristian's insurance policies for medical bills and her totaled car."

After three weeks in a coma, Kristian was transferred from the trauma hospital to an acute rehab facility. She still had rehabilitation to do to be considered fully emergent from a comatose state. Kristian's infant son had been released from the pediatric ICU and was recovering well. Her husband had sustained minor injuries that allowed him to care for both Kristian and their child. The doctors didn't know to what extent Kristian's injuries would inhibit basic human functions like being able to walk, talk, and remember again. But Kristian's team— her family and best friends—were laser-focused on helping Kristian get her life back.

The grip that once kept you and your best friend afloat as you launched off the inflatable inner tube is now the same grip that transcends all fear, and it never loses its force. When one end weakens, the other gets stronger, doing whatever is needed to rally behind her sister.

For Yana-Janell, this meant contacting breastfeeding moms— specifically those who had the same diet as Kristian—so she could help feed Kristian's infant son. It meant immediately and heroically helping in any way she could, along with other friends, to keep Kristian's company afloat while also managing her own public relations company. It meant documenting every step of Kristian's progress to remind her what she was capable of. Yana-Janell constantly reminded Kristian throughout her recovery, "I'm not tiptoeing around you. I'm talking to you the same way I talked to you before the accident. I'm talking to you like the same person because I expect that person to show up."

I spoke with Kristian almost a year to the day after her accident, and had I not seen a few articles on the accident, I would never have known she almost lost her life. I would never have known she had re-learned how to interpret and process information, let alone talk, remember, and walk up uneven surfaces.

"Those fears of stepping up onto a curb or down off of a curb existed," said Yana-Janell. "I told her 'Go ahead and go on your own time, I'll wait. Step out and fall or speak and if it doesn't come out right, who cares? I'm here with you the whole way.'" And Yana-Janell knew Kristian— her best friend and her sister—would overcome this.

> "She's always shown up. She's never met an obstacle she won't come up with a plan to conquer. Kristian is a visionary, ambitious as hell. She is an encourager, and she is fearless."

YANA-JANELL SCOTT

A year after Kristian's accident, she'd made substantial progress and was back leading her company's vision. Because of her accident, Kristian hired a lot of staff to help run BLK + GRN and moved to a fulfillment center in order to keep the business afloat. Almost a year to the day after her accident, Kristian was on stage performing in a pitch competition to win more capital for BLK + GRN, a moment she never thought would happen again. Kristian envisions BLK + GRN not only as a marketplace, but also as a company that one day would assist Black artisans to secure their supply chains and operations and enhance their marketing efforts. Kristian's ideas and visions have never stopped, even when she almost lost her life and had to learn how to talk again.

Sisterhood manifests itself in the littlest ways, and it's in these small moments that its power reveals itself. It's being there for your sister, helping her "put one foot in front of the other, moving inches at a time," as Yana-Janell said, and knowing that she will overcome whatever obstacle with you by her side. Maybe right now, she just needs your grip to be a little tighter and a little stronger.

SISTERS WHO DON'T LOOK LIKE YOU
My Sisterhood with Ashley Lyles began in 2013. I was a sports intern for her uncle, and he asked me and Ashley to help work the pre-award events for the ESPYS Awards, an awards show hosted by ESPN honoring the best college and professional athletes of the year. There was nothing special about our initial interaction, other than we were like two kids on a playground who said, *"I like you, you like me, let's best friends"* for those three days of work. Our last night working together—the night of the ESPYS Awards Ceremony—the iconic broadcaster, Robin Roberts, won the Arthur Ashe Award for Courage. Robin Roberts was a college basketball player at Southeastern Louisiana University, who had arrived at the school on a tennis scholarship. Robin pursued Sports Journalism and became an ESPN broadcaster for fifteen years before being inducted into the Women's Basketball Hall of Fame in 2012. She's currently the anchor of ABC's *Good Morning America.*

In 2008, Robin was diagnosed with breast cancer and underwent surgery and eight rounds of chemotherapy before being declared in remission. In 2012, she was diagnosed with myelodysplastic syndrome (MDC), a bone marrow disease. She spent the next year recovering from a bone marrow transplant and fighting the disease.[71] The Arthur Ashe Award reflects the attitude of the late Arthur Ashe who used his platform to advocate for human rights while publicly dealing with AIDS. The recipients of the Arthur Ashe award "possess strength in the face of adversity, courage in the face of peril and the willingness to stand up for their beliefs no matter what the cost."[72]

Then-First Lady Michelle Obama and Professional basketball player Lebron James introduced Robin and presented her with the award. In her acceptance speech, Robin said, "True strength isn't when you face down life's challenges on your own. It's when you take them on by accepting the help, faith, and love of others and knowing you are lucky to have those." Then, Robin looked out to the crowd, pointed, and said, "My big sister, Sally Anne, my [bone marrow] donor. I literally would not be here, heck, I wouldn't be standing anywhere, if it were not for you."[73]

As she said those words, Ashley and I linked our arms together and held on until we stood up to clap and wipe our tears after Robin's speech. We individually saw parts of ourselves in Robin. For me, Robin was an athlete who broke boundaries that once had prevented Black female athletes from excelling. She used that same courage to beat cancer and a blood disease. She used that same love she had

---

71 "Robin Roberts Biography," *A&E Television Networks: Biography,* April 16, 2020.

72 "About the Award: Arthur Ashe," *ESPN Internet Ventures,* date accessed March 2, 2021.

73 "Robin Roberts' Inspiring Award Acceptance Speech" *SportsCenterJSA,* July 18, 2013, video, 7:05.

for people to openly come out as gay and offer others the strength to love anyone they wanted to. She showed me and Ashley the importance and power of Sisterhood; whether you're blood-related or not, that Sisterhood could save someone's life in the way Yana-Janell helped save Kristian's.

The bond Ashley and I created in those three days turned into nearly a decade of Sisterhood living on opposite coasts. She was a three-sport athlete in college at Saint Mary's University in California before earning her MBA from the University of Southern California. Ashley is half Thai and half Black, four years older than me, and grew up with a single mother in Downtown LA. Though we're both from Southern California, our childhoods looked incredibly different. Our differences are special because we get to, like Kristian said, sit down and talk about hard things and understand where one another is coming from. We revel in and embrace what makes us who we are, and we support one another to pursue those ambitions. Because we've built our foundation on unconditional love and support for one another, we can have difficult conversations just as much as we can goof off.

SISTERHOOD IN THE WORKPLACE
Not all Sisterhood connections have to be incredibly powerful, like that of Yana-Janell and Kristian or Ashley and me. We can use the model of Sisterhood as a framework outside of our connections with our closest childhood friends. It shows us how to treat people with respect, to see them for who they individually are, and to create an environment where both are equitably supported. Research has shown that when "female leaders and entrepreneurs use the power of their work

Sisterhood, they are more confident and successful in the workplace."[74]

In order to be able to share this Sisterhood with one another, women need to understand where their sisters—especially their sisters who don't look like them—come from and how their experiences differ.

Two experts on Sisterhood relationships in and outside of the workplace are Ella Bell Smith, a Dartmouth College professor, and Stella Nkomo, a professor at the University of Pretoria and the President of the Africa Academy of Management (AFAM). In 2001, Ella and Stella co-authored a book called *Our Separate Ways,* which looks at the individual and collective struggles and triumphs of white women and women of color in the workplace. In Summer 2020, at the height of racial tension in America, *Harvard Business Review's* podcast, *Women at Work: Conversations about Women in Work Environments,* debuted a podcast called *Sisterhood is Critical to Racial Justice.*[75] The hosts interviewed Ella and Stella to talk about their nearly twenty-year-old book, the history of relationships between women and how America can start to strengthen the Sisterhood between women of different races.

Back in 2001, Ella and Stella surveyed eight hundred women and held in-depth interviews with 121 women, gathering information and analyzing different professional experiences

---

74 Terence Mauri, "Why Sisterhood Matters on International Women's Day," *Inc.*, March 8, 2018.

75 Amy Bernstein, Amy Galo, and Emily Caufield, "Sisterhood is Critical to Racial Justice," *Women at Work* by Harvard Business Review, June 8, 2020, podcast, Season 5, Episode 9, 64:59.

and relationships in the workplace between white women and women of color. The women they interviewed had entered the workforce in the 1970s and 1980s, the height of the women's liberation movement. Nearly twenty years later, Ella and Stella said that white and Black women were having similar experiences with one another in the workplace to the ones in the 70s and 80s. They found that feminism and racism—two largely different and incomparable experiences—were being treated as if they were one; when white women rose to the top, breaking through misogynistic barriers, they often didn't recognize that the color of their skin was preventing more women of color from sitting next to them or rising above them.

Ella and Stella found that white women had a glass ceiling, a barrier created by discrimination of gender, where they were able to see through to the top but prevented from getting there. Women of color not only had a ceiling formed by sexism but additionally had a concrete ceiling because of racism. Women of color were not only prevented from getting to the top but were prevented from seeing any possibility of what it was like to get there. Because of this, they couldn't see the one or two other women of color who bulldozed through the concrete ceiling, further perpetuating the importance of representation.

Had true Sisterhood been developed in the early 2000's, Ella and Stella argue that women's stance against misogyny and for equal opportunity now would not only be stronger, but there would also be more women of color in positions of power and more condemnation of racism. "While we espouse Sisterhood, I'm not sure if we *do* Sisterhood," said Ella.

"Part of the gaps that we see comes from naiveté about: 'Well, we are all in this together.'"[76]

In an earlier *HBR Women at Work* podcast called "Sisterhood is Power," Tina R. Opie, an associate professor of management at Babson College, and Verónica Caridad Rabelo, assistant professor of management in the College of Business at San Francisco State University, debut on the show.[77] Tina and Verónica specialize in studying women's relationships with one another in workplace environments, particularly how women form strong and meaningful relationships given their different backgrounds and ethnicities. Their goal for these studies is to understand how these bonds are formed and use these strategies to create "collective advancement" in the workplace. Collective advancement looks like getting women in higher positions at work; providing daycare for lower-level employees; noticing the intricacies where discrimination inserts itself and working to dismantle it; and even understanding that specific language might be triggering for different women.

Tina and Verónica expressed that over-optimism is a common sentiment women of color feel about their relationships with white women in the workplace—that simply a *"Hello!"* doesn't mean a close relationship. On the contrary, when looking further into what white women described as a good relationship, this high-level etiquette was often as far as white women went when investing in these relationships.

76 Joanna Piacenza, "Sisterhood in the Workplace Only Goes So Far When It Comes to Perceptions of Pay," *Morning Consult*, May 10, 2019.

77 Bernstein, Galo, and Caufield, "Sisterhood is Power," Season 2, Episode 10, 51:49.

Furthermore, because white women—more often than not in higher positions of power—didn't invest in relationships with women of color, they were less keen to noticing micro-aggressions in the workplace.[78] The idea of shared Sisterhood "allows us to share struggles together, realize that we're not alone, and that the pain we're going through is something bigger than us."[79]

From her research at BLK + GRN and talking to hundreds of Black business owners, Kristian has found minority women are starting their own businesses largely as a result of women of color having a very negative experience in the workplace. Kristian said, "My reason for thinking why that exists is because the workplace is so toxic for Black women." She added that Black women aren't seeing what they need for themselves in the market and what's representative of their culture, so they're making these products themselves.

Kristian said the founders she works with are not only over-whelmingly happier, but data proves they are incredibly suc-cessful; according to Minority Business Development Agency, the number of companies owned by minority women has grown 163 percent since 2007.[80] As of 2018, Women of Color account for 47 percent of all women-owned businesses. Addi-

---

78 Marguerite Ward and Rachel Premack, "What is a Microaggression? 14 Things People Think are Fine to Say at Work — but are Actually Racist, Sexist, or Offensive," *Business Insider*, July 24, 2020.

79 Beth A. Livingston and Tina R. Opie, "Even at 'Inclusive' Companies, Women of Color Don't Feel Supported," *Harvard Business Review*, August 29, 2018.

80 "The Number of Firms Owned by Minority Women has Grown 163% since 2007," Minority Business Development Agency, U.S. Department of Commerce, blog, August 2018.

tionally, 5.82 million of these businesses employ 2.22 million people and generate $386.6 million in revenue. The report also suggests that if revenues generated by minority women-owned firms matched those generated by all women-owned businesses, four million new jobs would be added and surpass $1.2 trillion in revenue for the US economy.[81]

Kristian said we need a "coming to Jesus moment," where Black people can explain why they feel white people are hostile and people can have a better understanding of the actions that are causing this. She acknowledges, "This problem is a complicated one. I think we have to help people get more comfortable using their power to be anti-racist."

The Sisterhood model teaches us to have unconditional love for our women, despite growing up and looking different. It reminds us that relationships built from a place of compassion have the power to bring life where there is suffering. When we build a foundation on Sisterhood—seeing someone for how they want to be seen, who they are, and not defining them by the color of their skin or their class—we are actually linking arms to send our collective kinetic energy to one another. We can support one another's rise into positions of power especially as women grow their own businesses and continually fight to disband the sexist and racist systems that oppress our sisters. If we see our differences as an advantage and not as a means of separation, we can combine our strengths, become one another's grips, and accomplish anything.

---

81 Ibid.

CHAPTER 11

THE RISE AND FALL OF FEMALE LEADERS

BEWARE OF GLASS CLIFFS

The city is under destruction and fires light up everywhere. Rubble and crushed buildings decorate the once effervescent metropolitan city. People are running frantically, their faces marred by the color of ashes. Fear-stricken, they stumble to safety. The camera focuses on the villain with slimy flesh spotted with moldy wounds sporting an evil grin that reveals the black tar cemented onto its teeth. The villain glides over the ant-sized humans below, suffocating them with the gastric slime secreted out from its tail.

The next morning, people watch the news petrified, as the journalists cry out, "Where's our Superhero?" They pray for a supernatural phenomenon to appear from its hiding place and save the city. These are the same citizens who suppressed this Superhero into hiding when the Superhero failed to save 100 percent of the people. Now, they yearn for the Superhero's help.

It's this very Superhero archetype that famously manifests itself today in many of the Fortune 500 companies, an annual ranking of the top revenue-producing companies, among other conglomerates. They call in the Superhero when the company is losing revenue, not hitting key benchmarks, and failing. No, wait. They call in the woman.

In 2005, University of Exeter researchers, Michelle Ryan and Alexander Haslam, conducted a study on one hundred companies listed on the London Stock Exchange. They were fact-checking an article in *The Times* that said women leaders negatively impacted company performance. They compared the performance of the companies mentioned to periods of overall market decline. They found the companies that brought on women board members had a consistent decline in company performance as much as five months before. Michelle and Alexander labeled this term the glass cliff. "The glass cliff is a phenomenon whereby women and people of other minority groups are more likely to occupy positions of leadership that are risky and precarious," said Michelle. "This can happen when share price performance is poor, when facing a scandal, or when the role involves reputational risk."[82]

Utah State University researchers Alison Cook and Christy Glass continued Michelle and Alexander's study by analyzing Fortune 500 companies over a span of fifteen years. They, too, found that white women and people of color were likelier to see a promotion to CEO of poorly performing companies.[83]

---

82 Emily Stewart, "Why Struggling Companies Promote Women: The Glass Cliff, Explained," *Vox*, October 31, 2018.

83 Ibid.

When this woman Superhero throws her iconic fist in the air and is promoted to the top, we say she shatters the glass ceiling. This very glass ceiling represents the seemingly invisible but poignantly felt bias a woman experiences because of her gender. Once she breaks through the ceiling, shards of the glass lie everywhere and, finally, she has made it. However, no one sweeps up those shards of glass. Rather, their sharp edges stab the Superhero woman as she strives to revive the failing company. All the while, the piercing edges push her to the precipice of the ceiling, which has melted away with last year's hope of having a female executive. Finally, she's shoved off the glass cliff, excused from her position.

One woman who has experienced the glass cliff phenomenon is Carol Bartz. She became the first woman CEO of Yahoo! in January 2009 after the 2008 financial crisis when Yahoo! laid off sixteen hundred employees. Two and a half years later, Bartz was fired.[84] The company chose the then-CFO of Yahoo, Timothy Morse, to be the interim CEO.

In 2012, Yahoo! hired Marissa Mayer as their CEO, after reducing their staff by 14 percent and experiencing four turnovers in leadership in less than a year. Mayer was forced out in 2017 and eventually replaced by a white man who made double her salary.[85]

In 2018, JCPenney chose Jill Soltau—former President and CEO of the fabric and craft store retailer, Joann—as CEO.

84   Lydia Dishman, "What is the Glass Cliff, and Why Do So Many Female CEOs Fall Off It?" *Fast Company*, July 27, 2018.

85   Buster Coen, "11 Critical Moments from Marissa Mayer's Rocky Time as Yahoo's CEO," *The Street*, June 13, 2017.

JCPenney had already been on an eight-year decline that started in 2010 when its sales had dropped by 10 percent from reported earnings in 2006.[86] Finally, in May 2020, JCPenney filed for bankruptcy after over a century of business and having made a name as one of America's largest department stores.

As of 2020, only 6.6 percent—or thirty seven—of the Fortune 500 companies have a female CEO, and only three of those women are women of color.[87] Women jump at less-than-ideal opportunities because it may be the only chance they get to prove themselves. However, when they fail with the odds stacked against them, they're cast as unable to perform the job and a major part of the company's failure. In reality, women were never actually given a fighting chance. You can lead a horse to water but you can't make it drink, right? But what if there's no water for them to begin with? These women are led to these opportunities and decide to jump into them headfirst, but they're given no resources and no solid ground to stand on. Of course, they can't prove themselves.

In another fifteen-year study, research showed that a female CEO succeeded another female CEO in only four of 608 transitions at Fortune 500 companies. This same research found what so many others had: that occupational minorities—white women and women of color—were more likely to be hired at a poorly performing company. When the

86 Bethany Biron, "The 118-Year Rise and Fall of JCPenney, One of America's Largest Department Stores," *Business Insider*, May 15, 2020.

87 Susanne Bruckmüller and Nyla R. Branscombe, "How Women End Up on the 'Glass Cliff'," *Harvard Business Review: January - February Edition*, 2011.

performance of the company declined under these women, white men were hired as their replacements, a result which the research calls "the savior effect."[88]

The first thing we need to do is to get rid of the glass ceiling altogether. If there's no glass ceiling, then there's no glass cliff. While we're working hard to dismantle and rebuild hundreds of years' worth of systems that built the thick layers of glass ceilings, we need to reconsider the expectation of the individual we're putting in charge of the company—do they best represent what the company needs, or are they just someone whom we can blame? A woman is fit to revive a suffering company, but she should be provided at least as many resources and as much support as her predecessor.

The woman Superhero is the incarnation of resilience, compassion, and power all folded into one. A woman shouldn't just be given the leading executive role when the company is suffering, but also when it's thriving. When we put women in situations that will allow her to thrive, we'll find renewed hope not just in the bottom line, but also for the humanity of individuals. She represents a new vision of joy and fulfillment as a leader who cares about her team of employees and their well-being. However, she can't do this if she's being shoved off a glass cliff. She should be *believed in*, not pushed to her demise.

She shouldn't be called in to clean an impossible mess; rather, she should be called in to *start a revolution*.

---

88 Allison Cook and Christy Glass, "Above the Glass Ceiling: When are Women and Racial / Ethnic Minorities Promoted to CEO?" *Wiley Online Library*, published June 10, 2013.

DEMISE OF THE GIRLBOSS

After seeing their mothers and grandmothers fight and suffer through deceiving and unforgiving glass ceilings and glass cliffs, many Millennial women wanted to imagine and build a different social and corporate structure. They wanted one that didn't stifle and deprecate women, but instead one that was built by women for all women.

In 2013, Sophia Amoruso tried to rebuild what she most likely thought was the answer to creating a new feminist structure, which she called the "Girlboss." Until 2020, Girlboss reigned as a new type of pop-culture feminism. Sophia was the founder and CEO of Nasty Gal, a vintage clothing company that, at its peak, made over $300 million in annual sales. She started Nasty Gal in 2006 as a community college dropout working a minimum wage job. With a passion for vintage clothing and an eye for opportunity, Sophia created a flourishing eBay site where she would resell vintage designer clothing at a marked-up price. Just two years after launch, Nasty Gal turned into a vintage-inspired retailer, selling hidden vintage gems of clothing and more provocative styles from renowned designers that resonated with the rebellious Nasty Gal audience.[89] After six years in business, Nasty Gal had over two hundred employees, hit $100 million in revenue, and Sophia was labeled "fashion's new phenom."[90]

In 2014, Sophia wrote her autobiography called *#Girlboss* about her driven, fear-evasive, and rebellious self. She

---

89 Nicole Perlroth, "Naughty in Name Only," *The New York Times*, March 24, 2013.

90 Victoria Barret, "Nasty Gal's Sophia Amoruso: Fashion's New Phenom," *Forbes*, June 28, 2012.

immediately became a *New York Times* best-seller and *Girl-boss* became a Netflix TV Series in 2017. The Girlboss mentality caught the attention of predominantly white Millennial women and tried to propel an evolved type of feminism that told women they were the boss of their own lives.[91] In 2015, Sophia stepped down from her CEO position at Nasty Gal, saying "I didn't love having eight people reporting to me and asking me over and over if we're hitting targets. I'm a creative. I'm a brand-builder. I'm a rainmaker. I'm a pretty good marketer, but that's not something I want to do every day."[92] At the company's peak, Sophia's net worth was estimated to be around $280 million. After mismanagement, Nasty Gal filed for bankruptcy in 2016 and eventually sold for $20 million.[93]

Sophia bounced back from the bankruptcy and turned her *#Girlboss* book into Girlboss Media in 2017, a content company with the purpose of spreading women empowerment through events, digital media, and social media.[94] The term and mentality of Girlboss quickly transpired into marketing material and messages from women to women in corporate offices, start-ups, and among friend groups. In 2019, Sophia sold Girlboss Media to Attention Capital while remaining its CEO until 2020 when she announced her departure from

---

91 Leigh Stein, "The End of the Girlboss is Here," *Medium: Gen*, June 22, 2020.

92 Clare O'Connor, "As Nasty Gal Files Bankruptcy, Founder Sophia Amoruso's Fortune Decimated," *Forbes*, November 11, 2016.

93 Sissi Cao, "A Conversation with Sophia Amoruso, the 'Girlboss' Founder of Nasty Gal," *Observer*, October 2, 2018.

94 Ibid.

Girlboss Media, possibly as a result of decelerating revenue during the COVID-19 pandemic.[95]

Journalists declared that the Girlboss era was officially over upon Sophia's departure. I personally noticed the fade of Girlboss lingo and branded memorabilia among my friend groups not long after it took off in 2017. My friends and I realized the fluff seemed more like a short-term pep-talk for a promotion discussion but didn't actually move women closer to being equal.[96]

My intention isn't to take down other women for my own benefit by sharing the Girlboss history. Instead, my intention is to understand what worked and what didn't during the Girlboss era and why it wasn't a successful social construct for women. From the outside, it appeared Sophia bootstrapped and built two different successful companies. There's no way of knowing all of the facts without actually interviewing everyone involved, especially Sophia. However, as a consumer, I can speak to what I know and felt about the Girlboss movement.

At the beginning, I believed in this Girlboss movement. I was in my latter years of college when it built momentum. I remember marching down to the Washington, DC National Mall for the first-ever Women's March in 2017 with #Girlboss etched in bold sharpie on my cardboard poster. In that moment, with hundreds of thousands of women, girls, boys,

95 Lydia Dishman, "It's the End of an Era for #Girlboss as Founder and CEO Sophia Amoruso Steps Down," *Fast Company*, June 22, 2020.

96 Amanda Mull, "The Girlboss Has Left the Building," *The Atlantic*, June 25, 2020.

and men, I felt like a girl boss, protesting and speaking out for women's rights and equality. At this time, I also witnessed the surge of Girlboss messaging and memorabilia among my friends and new female-founded companies inspired by Girlboss Media and Sophia Amoruso's rise to power. Girlbossery had become a hot trend, an aesthetic, and a way of speaking. However being a Girlboss seemed like a momentary fight for power that centered yourself as an individual in the workplace. Milestones of true equality, like women's reproductive health, family planning, and equal pay, were tangentially tacked on as a marketing ploys. Women's equality was never the center of the movement—individual power was.

To me, Girlbossery meant always fighting to gain the power from those who had it—white men—only to exercise your power *over* people who didn't have it—other women and women of color. This is why I believe the Girlboss era that began in 2013 to shake up the patriarchy came to an end just seven years later.

Slowly, starting in December of 2019 and lasting through July 2020, the following female founders and executives of companies that thrived during the Girlboss era were forced to resign or step down "amid allegations of toxic work cultures that perpetuated racism:"

- Away co-founder and CEO, Steph Korey, stepped down
- Outdoor Voices founder and CEO, Ty Haney, resigned
- Refinery 29 editor-in-chief and co-founder, Christine Barberich, resigned
- Man Repeller founder, Leandra Medine, stepped back to an intern role

- Ban.Do co-founder and Chief Creative Officer, Jen Glotch, resigned after a leave of absence
- The Wing co-founder and CEO, Audrey Gelman, resigned
- Reformation founder and CEO, Yael Aflalo, stepped down[97]

Girlbossery never got rid of the glass ceilings or glass cliffs. Women founders and executives created companies so they could rise to the top without facing glass ceilings in their own company. But the power-hungry Girlboss era posed a question that many of these women leaders in power faced: "How do we treat people well while still running a successful company?" Like generations before them, the women mentioned above were shoved off of glass cliffs, unable to repair their wrongs. Some of these leaders should have been given a chance to admit their mistakes and take action to make sure they and others didn't commit the same ones.

What seemingly started as a way to re-create a system into one representative of fairness and camaraderie was really an unstable foundation borrowed from the most successful white male leaders against whom white women wanted revenge. It was an attitude filled with hate instead of focusing on working together as a team. Revenge is not synonymous with change or transformation, but instead, permeates into the way we treat each other and leaves us hurting one another. The Girlboss movement made feminism a cool social-climbing circle instead of a necessity to advocate for

---

97 Hillary Hoffower, "The Fall of the Girlboss is Actually a Good Thing," *Business Insider*, July 26, 2020.

women—especially BIPOC women, LGTBQ women and femmes, and those hyper-marginalized by society.

I want to reimagine and rebuild a reality with a diverse set of women in order to understand what links are missing between us and how we can equitably amend them. I want to stand for more than being successful at my job, because that doesn't define me. What defines me are the multifaceted talents I have, my imperfections, and my excellence that I can bring. What defines me are my superpowers and how I choose to use them to elevate not just women, but everyone around me. Of course, we should work to achieve the best positions we can, but the way we get there and the foundation on which we stand should be the priority.

There's a way for women to lead by having all the attributes needed to run a successful business—work ethic, confidence, adaptability, and relentlessness—without also repurposing the very barriers that have held women back from assuming higher roles. Instead of competing with the systems that have doomed us for failure, we should reimagine a different future: a world of Superheroes who constantly rebuild themselves so they can bring out the uniqueness in others and create what we see together without individualism, oppression, or suffering.

We should constantly fight for what is best for collective groups of women rather than individual agendas. And when we make mistakes, which we will, we should listen and learn so we can grow into better people—like phoenixes rising from the ashes.

Women are way more than Girlbosses or a moment in time fighting for a top position. We should strive to be Superheroes—a forever commitment and action to bring out the best in ourselves and others.

CHAPTER 12

INVEST IN HUMAN CAPITAL

A Superhero's legacy is measured by the amount of collective impact they have on the lives of individuals. Tangible resources such as money can have a substantial impact on someone's life, but those alone cannot help someone discover their unique superpowers and elevate them in a way they couldn't have otherwise imagined. Rather, it's the intangible resources, like your human investment in someone unquantifiable by numbers, that are the essence of Superheroism and the reason why it continues on. By believing in someone—an act that can't be seen but can be deeply felt—we show people what they're uniquely capable of. Belief in someone shows them they have the ability to achieve their goals, and providing resources for that person is a commitment to that belief.

However, if we invest resources in someone before we believe in them, we risk having power over that person and suppressing them because we're the hand that has made them prosper.

Superheroism cannot exist when people are oppressed. When we believe in individuals before we provide resources, we don't think about power over them though our investments. Rather, we think of power as amplifying what they've made themselves and using our combined strengths to generate a formidable team.

This is why human capital—your people—is the greatest investment you can make, whether you're on a sports team, in the army, or investing in future billion-dollar companies.

GOING INTO BATTLE

Koma Gandy Fischbein is the Vice President of Curriculum for Codecademy, an educational company committed to developing and making modern learning technology like coding widely accessible. When she's not developing curriculum for more than 25 million users, Koma is the head coach of the Navy Men's Rugby team. In 2020, her alma mater Harvard University asked Koma to be the Chief Marshal at their 369th Commencement. The Harvard Alumni Association President Alice Hill said, "Koma Gandy Fischbein's dedication to service—to her country, to her community, and to Harvard—is an admirable example of the power of giving back. In pursuing her passions, she strives to transform the lives of others, whether it's through rugby, music, or her commitment to veterans."[98]

---

98 "Koma Gandy Fischbein '95 Elected Chief Marshal," *The Harvard Gazette*, February 13, 2020.

At an early age, Koma fell in love with sports, which translated into the self-discipline she worked to foster her entire life. When she arrived at Harvard, Koma played on the Women's Varsity Soccer team for two years before joining the rugby team for her last two years. Little did she know, her passion for rugby would turn into a twenty-year career that included multiple call-ups to compete for a spot on the USA Women's National Rugby Team. Koma has continued her love for rugby not only through coaching but also by promoting rugby among girls and women through the Sierra Leone Rugby Union and in underserved communities through Play Rugby USA. Rugby gave Koma a gateway to people-centric leadership, which taught her "it's not about being the best. It's just about being valued."

In addition to attending one of the top universities in the world and playing a sport, Koma was also enrolled in the Navy Reserve Officer Training Corps (NROTC). When Koma graduated from Harvard in 1993, she went straight into the Navy. At the time, there were very few women in officer roles, let alone women of color like Koma. The combat moratorium had just been lifted, which meant that women could serve on combat ships that were not previously open to them. Koma says her position as a female leader and Black woman "put me under a lot of pressure because there's sort of a view of what leadership looks like." She said, "I was almost a deviation from the norm because I didn't look like or lead like what my sailors were used to, which was very male-centric and white leadership."

She first had to figure out how she would lead her teams with a style that made them believe in her. Koma told me,

"There's no one model of leadership. It's a model that you have to adapt to yourself. If it's not authentic, it's not going to work." For Koma, that looked like letting her sailors know her authentic self and approaching leadership with a people-centric view. She asked about their families, their hobbies, and made a point to know what made them, *them*. She baked for them while they were out at sea, showing her team that she genuinely cared for them while also allowing them to get to know a different side of her through something she loved. Some people dismissed her baking as being stereotypical of a woman's role, but in the end, Koma says, "It's about the empowerment that you give people to express themselves," and acknowledging even little things like someone's enjoyment of baking.

It was not only in Koma's nature to get to know others, but Koma knew that she and her sailors were going to be put into life-sacrificing positions, and it was paramount to her that she garnered their trust. Koma's experience as a Naval Officer and leading a team on the rugby field complemented each other. About both the Navy and the game of rugby, Koma said, "If you don't get the trust and respect of your people, they're not going to trust the direction that you're leading them to go."

Koma finished her career in the Navy after having served an immediate deployment during the start of the Iraq War, achieving the rank of Lieutenant Commander, and earning a Navy Commendation Medal, three Navy Achievement Medals, and a US Coast Guard Meritorious Unit Commendation, among other awards.

In 2019, Koma became the head coach of the Navy Men's Rugby team, making her the first-ever female coach of a men's Armed Forces sports team. She was entering another circumstance in which she was the first female but had expectations to conform to the same coaching style as her male coach colleagues. Koma learned to adapt to the environment while still remaining effective and authentic to her individual abilities.

However, this didn't come immediately for Koma when she became the men's coach. She recalls being in a hotel room before one of her first games at her first Armed Forces tournament as head coach. She had seen a number of the other head coaches that day who gave her confused looks with eyes that asked, *"What are you doing here?"* She faced herself in the mirror as thoughts of self-doubt ran through her head. She asked herself, *"Should I be modeling myself after this type of coach or that type of coach?"*

She reached out to coaches whom she respected and who knew her style. They said, "You're going to be fine. Keep doing what you're doing. Coaches are going to make mistakes. You don't have to know everything. Just be yourself." She turned to what she knew made her successful in the Navy; she focused on getting to know her athletes, showing she believed in them, and treated them as human beings instead of just athletes.

"I don't believe that you can effectively lead a team if you're not invested in them. Giving a s*** about the people who you're coaching or who you're leading is the most important thing."

KOMA GANDY FISCHBEIN

Now, as Vice President of Curriculum for Codeacademy, Koma understands the amount she invests in standing by her people directly impacts the success of the products her team creates. Koma said, "If I don't know that one of my curriculum developers is struggling, for example, because her grandma is sick, then I failed. If my people aren't coming to me with a problem, then I failed. If we don't know people on a fundamental level and value them as individuals, how can we expect them to fight next to us in war?"

Koma also told me, "If we don't value the color of their skin, and if we don't value the fact that they're treated differently in this world, how are we going to expect them to trust that we have their back no matter what? My focus is really about the challenge of motivating groups of people that I'm privileged enough to lead to get us to someplace better tomorrow than we were today."

Koma's achievements are almost unheard of. She has achieved the pinnacles of success in three different industries, yet she remains one of the humblest individuals I've ever spoken to. Her Superheroism is defined by what she does to elevate her sailors, athletes, technological employees, and, in turn, her accomplishments follow. She teaches us that investing in your people regardless of your scenario is an element that not only could save their lives in war, but also can help them become Superheroes themselves.

PENNY CHECKS

Investing in human capital on every team, from the Navy to venture capital, means being an authentic leader whose actions and intentions are rooted in valuing their team members as individuals.

Jesse Draper is a fourth-generation venture capitalist, but the first female one in her family. She looked up to her dad in the venture industry, and he taught her everything he knew about venture capital, from technology to start-ups to investing. At the time, she didn't see many—if any—women who were venture capitalists. So, she said to herself, "*Oh but men do that, I can't do that.*"

"As any little girl does, you look at what women around you are doing," Jesse told me. Inspired by her aunt, Polly Draper, a successful actress and screenwriter with an Emmy nomination and a Screen Actor's Guild Award, Jesse turned to entertainment. She attended UCLA School of Theater, Film and Television. After graduation, she starred in a Nickelodeon show, *The Naked Brothers Band* and appeared in a number of movies.

She realized her heart was in technology and innovation after going to the first-ever Twitter conference in Los Angeles. Her gut told her, "*This is what I really want to do. I want to go into technology.*" Yet, she still thought she couldn't do what her dad and her male family members had done because she was female.

As a bridge to cross into her desired field, Jesse blended acting and technology to create, produce, and star in *The Valley Girl Show*, a web series and technology talk show. On this show, she interviewed the most creative and technologically advanced entrepreneurs and tech geniuses, asking them questions about themselves, their companies, and the future of tech. At the time, social media was on the precipice of booming, and Google was quickly becoming the new tech giant.

Living in Los Angeles showed Jesse that people wanted to see entertainment celebrities on the covers of magazines rather than the tech entrepreneurs who she had idolized growing up. But she chose to see this as an opportunity to find women in the tech space and amplify their image. Jesse said, "I initially felt like I couldn't go into technology because I didn't see women in technology. I need to get more women in technology on my show."

Finding women in tech to interview was difficult for Jesse and her team. Jesse said, "In those early days, I was dying for female mentors and advisors." She approached women in fashion technology to come onto her show, like Jennifer Hyman, co-founder and CEO of Rent the Runway, a technology and logistics company that allows women to rent luxury and designer clothing, as well as fashion handbag and clothing designer Rebecca Minkoff. Once she had these reputable women on her show, other women also wanted to come on. Soon, both women and men in high power positions in the tech world reached out to Jesse. She subsequently interviewed Sheryl Sandberg, COO of Facebook, Mark Cuban, entrepreneur and Dallas Mavericks owner, Aneesh Chopra, the first CTO of the United States of America, and Sandra Day O'Connor, the first female justice of the United States Supreme Court. Jesse also built a new tech site and acquired a technology blog in LA called Lalawag. Little did she know, *The Valley Girl Show* would be nominated for an Emmy award in 2015 and go on to produce over three hundred interviews, maintaining a 50-50 balance of women to men.

While producing and hosting *The Valley Girl Show*, many founders and executives of start-ups would want to appear on her show. These companies were often too young for the show, but Jesse would redirect them to her network of investors in Silicon Valley. Jesse was amassing a ton of investment through her interviews and learning what a good and bad deal looked like. She began writing penny checks, investing whatever she could into companies where she saw a market opportunity or met a founder she believed in. After building enough momentum, Jesse created her venture capital firm, Halogen Ventures, in 2016.

BREATHING FIRE
The Valley Girl Show not only proved to Jesse how passionate she was about tech and solidified her knack for finding great investments, but it also helped Jesse find women in tech and provide them with the resources they needed to succeed. As of 2021, Halogen invested in sixty-two women-founded or women-led companies. In their first-ever fundraising effort,

Halogen Ventures raised $10 million from investors that Jesse and her team would use to invest in female founded start-ups.

Jesse and her team at Halogen Ventures are on a mission to prove that investing in women is a massive business opportunity because these women-founded companies are making returns. Jesse said, "Just because I invest in women-led and women-founded companies, that doesn't mean I'm running a non-profit."[99]

In fall 2020, Jesse wrote an op-ed called, "Investing in Women Isn't a F***ing Charity."[100] Within a month, this article received over a million hits and garnered attention from renowned national television news sources. In this article, Jesse describes returning home late to LA from a taxing business trip in NYC, desperately wanting to embrace her husband and two young children, kick her heels off, and relax. Right as she got home, she received a call to meet an investor for dinner who could potentially help with Halogen's second fundraise.

She changed quickly after kissing her kids and went to dinner, only to be one of the only women at a table with older white men who openly admitted to being drunk and high after a day on the golf course and weren't discreet when scheduling prostitutes to meet them in their hotel rooms after dinner. Not being taken seriously and being disrespected was all too familiar for Jesse while being in the technology and venture capital space.

---

99 Jesse Draper, "Investing in Women Isn't a Fucking Charity," *Medium*, September 28, 2020.
100 Ibid.

Often, without giving Jesse a chance, men who hold the financial resources to invest in women's ventures have said to Jesse and her team, "Hey cutie, women founders isn't a big enough market," "Don't they all end up having babies and quitting?" "There are too many cat fights," or "There's not enough deal flow because no women are starting companies."[101] The stigma that has perpetuated the notion that women are unfit for entrepreneurship continues to persist at the funding level—the very place Jesse and her team are trying to dismantle and reconfigure.

Jesse said, "When we don't control how we invest at the funding level, the bottom may never change. It means we put fewer products out into the world that improve the lives of women, BIPOC, and marginalized communities." As of 2020, only 7 percent of women are in venture capital, and 1 percent are BIPOC women.[102]

After having many successful exits where Jesse and her team decided to liquidate their stake in a company, I asked Jesse how she knows who to invest in and which companies will be successful. Though she hasn't gathered concrete data, she said she bets on a personality type.

She said, "I look for women who can breathe fire and walk through walls. *No* doesn't affect them—they're insanely optimistic. Their bank accounts might be empty, but it doesn't matter. The company will continue. They're all heads down. Work, work, work." Jesse reflected, "They're kind of quiet.

---

101 Jesse Draper, "Investing in Women Isn't a Fucking Charity," *Medium*, September 28, 2020.

102 Ibid.

They don't need to be the star. The company is the star they just want to build. And that has been the best personality type for me."

Jesse said coachable founders are the best because they realize founding and building a company isn't linear, but rather similar to carrying a bag of rocks up a mountain. When they arrive at the peak, then they go and try to climb another mountain, facing adversity head-on whenever it comes across them. She told me, "I look for women who can think really big. They're building billion-dollar businesses and respond to any question with, *'I think we could try that if we did it this way.'*"

In 2020, Jesse and her team of two saw over five thousand deals. In the beginning of 2021, they raised a $21 million fund and had invested in sixty-two start-ups, all honoring Halogen's mission of investing in companies that have at least one female founder.

"*Invest* in women. We're not a f***ing charity. We're a $3 Trillion Opportunity."[103]

JESSE DRAPER

At the end of the day, Jesse is investing in female leaders who she believes have products that will transform the lives of consumers. She and her team's investments are their commitments—their confidence and overwhelming support—in

---

103 Ibid.

these individual women leaders, telling them, *"You got this, and I'm here for you."* From the outside, this support may look different than Koma's, but the means is the same. They both cherish the connection they have with individual team members and use their positions to elevate these individuals.

As you are creating your team, whether that be a project team, a founding team, or any other type of team, I encourage you to get to know each one of your people and establish a strong foundation with them. Figure out what makes them tick and how you can help elevate them. Never underestimate the power and impact of your daily actions. When you invest in your people, they will invest in themselves and continue the forward momentum.

CHAPTER 13

DEFINE YOUR
SUPERPOWERS

OUTSIDE BACK

Mary was two years my senior when I arrived at Georgetown, and I immediately gravitated toward her 6'0" stature the first day of preseason. I knew she understood me. Our Irish coach who was confident in his humor, dubbed us "Giant 1 and Giant 2." If we were lucky, he called us "The Surfboards." The second day on campus, we ran a fitness test called the Man U's, short for Manchester United. To pass, we had to complete twenty-one consecutive sprints 120 yards long. We had to make each consecutive sprint in one second faster until we arrived at fifteen seconds. Once we reached fifteen second sprints, every sprint after that had to be within fifteen seconds. Every minute on the minute, we sprinted. We used the remaining seconds of each one-minute block to jog back to the starting line. If we made it to twenty-seven sprints, we hit what we called "Target," and we didn't have to run the subsequent two fitness tests.

My freshman year, when I lined up for the Man U's, Mary jogged over to line up next to me. As a nervous freshman, my immediate thought was she was trying to race me, but instead she said, "Let's do this, Marines. We're both crushing this." I exhaled a massive sigh of relief. Well into the fitness test, when I was jogging back from sprint twenty-four, I started to lose control of my legs. They were moving, but it seemed the instructions from my brain to my legs were about five seconds too slow. *Faster* my brain commanded, and slowly my legs followed. I had three more sprints until I hit Target.

Mary, who had stopped at sprint twenty-two, jumped back on the line. I looked at her and shouted "Mary, what are you doing?" in the way you do when you're exhausted and have to pump words out of your stomach. She enthusiastically and confidentially responded, "I'm running with you to make sure you hit Target." She ran the last three sprints with me, for no other reason but to help me. Conserving her energy for our other fitness tests and hefty training camp schedule or feeling sorry for herself for stopping weren't her concerns. She wanted *me* to succeed more than she cared about herself.

That was the beginning of our Sisterhood, and I looked up to her in every way as an athlete, student, and woman. She's Minnesotan, and it felt like she demonstrated "the nicest people in the country" Midwestern stereotype. When I tore my ACL, her mother made me a homemade blanket that I still sleep with every night to remind me I have the love and strength of the Kroening family to make it through. When I moved to New York City after graduation, Mary was my rock who introduced me to the Village Tavern Irish bar with the best Guinness and made me feel like NYC could be my home. I knew I was safe there because my big sister was there.

In 2021, Mary became a finalist for a prestigious leadership award by Ernst & Young (EY), a multinational professional services firm commonly known for being one of "Big 4" accounting firms in the US.[104] Each year, EY nominates high-performing managers who have exhibited exceptional leadership, performance, and success in their roles in the financial services industry to apply for a membership in the Women's Bond Club Rising Star Award program.[105] Mary had worked there since she graduated from college in 2014. She earned a sponsorship from EY to earn her Master's in Business Administration (MBA) from University of Pennsylvania's Wharton School of Business, tied with Stanford as the number one ranked MBA program in the country as of 2020.[106]

In typical Mary fashion, she doesn't know how wonderful she is. Her superpowers are her unforgiving hard work and the sense of self-confidence she gives to other people. When Mary asked me what she should write when EY nominated her to apply for the Women's Bond Club Rising Star Award, she also mentioned she was surprised she was chosen to apply. I laughed and said, "Mary, what do you mean? You represent leadership in every sense of the word." She replied shyly, "Thanks, Marines. I don't know ..."

---

104 Will Kenton, "What is the Big 4," *Investopedia,* January 7, 2021.
105 "Rising Star Award," Women's Bond Club, accessed March 2, 2021.
106 "2021 Best Business Schools," *US News,* 2020.

Many of us—if you haven't been already—will be asked, "What are your strengths? What are you good at? How would you describe yourself?" What the prompt or people are really asking, is, "What are your *superpowers?*"

Mary decided to use her experience playing in the position of an outside back in soccer to guide her through the prompt. The outside back position is one of the most unselfish positions on the field. Outside backs are not only responsible for attacking and assisting the team in scoring goals, but they're also responsible for being a crucial part to the defense, assisting the team from being scored on. They are constantly running despite having a low chance of getting the ball. Often, their runs will take the opponent out of position, opening up other players on the attack.

Outside backs like Mary will run the extra three sprints with you even though it serves them no personal benefit.

Mary shared her submission to Ernst & Young with me. She wrote, "Beneath my plain black work uniform are the superpowers of an outside back. While my official role as co-captain and defender of a Division I soccer team ended in 2014, I have carried the outside back mentality, leadership qualities, and skillset forward to my professional career at EY."

Then, eloquently and boldly, she described in the next three paragraphs how each of the roles of an outside back transpired to her role as a successful manager. She has been tasked with roles at work designed for people ten years her senior, and she has merged groups who traditionally had animosity between them. She closed her submission with, "While I've swapped my cleats in my backpack for multiple laptops, the superpowers of an outside back remain in me, enabling me to lead by example with integrity and excellence."

BORN WITH IT

Often without thinking, our superpowers are at play. I think superpowers are a part of our natural design, but it's our decision whether or not we listen to our gut, tap into them, and use them. Have you ever had the feeling, *"I don't know why, but my gut is telling me to act in this particular way"*? Our gut is the queen of our superpowers because it holds our truth—what we know is right, deep within our souls.

Your gut may tell you:

"Choose your fight." Combat your inner monsters and find the people and causes you want to spend your life fighting for.

"Believe in yourself." You're born worthy.

"Be resilient." Get back up on the balance beam.

"Be a good teammate." Spread sticky notes, not hate.

"Be a sister." Relentlessly love and stand up for women you believe in.

"Lead yourself." Find a place of inner security and individuality.

"Lead for the people." Invest your superpowers in people who breathe fire.

"Be a motivator." Inspire people to find their unique super-powers.

"Become a Superhero." Use your superpowers to lift yourself and others to inconceivable places.

We must learn how to listen to our gut instinct, and we must honor what it tells us. From there, we can unpack our superpowers. Through life experiences and choosing how to respond to situations, we can foster the superpowers within ourselves. Once we take the time to do so, we actually can accomplish the unbelievable—like getting into one of the top universities in the world or building a million-dollar company.

Marilou McFarlane has spent her career listening to her gut, and it has led her to live her most fulfilled life. In turn, the product of her work has opened avenues for other people to harness their superpowers and go after roles they otherwise wouldn't because they don't see other people like them.

Marilou is the founder of Women in Sports Tech (WiST) and a former collegiate cross-country athlete at the University of North Carolina (UNC) Chapel Hill. After working in various leadership roles for sports tech start-ups for about ten years, she was increasingly frustrated to be the only woman in meetings other than those she herself had hired. The blend of her passions—sports, technology, and female empowerment—inspired her to eventually found WiST in 2017, a nonprofit company designed to connect more women with sports technology career opportunities.

Earlier in her career, Marilou was mentoring two young women, both esteemed college athletes from University of North Carolina and the University of Pennsylvania. They both were interested in the sports tech opportunities Marilou had described to them but didn't know how to apply or find open roles. They especially didn't see women in the technology space. At the time, Marilou was the CEO of Edufii (now known as CoachNow) and focused on sports technology designed to help coaches make a bigger impact and communicate more effectively with their athletes. She recognized there was a gender discrepancy in technology, as she was most often the only woman in the room. She said, "We love enlightened white men—I'm married to one—so how can we help them diversify their teams for better results and greater innovation?" This multigenerational story, from leading two young women to accomplishing gender equity at every age in sports and technology, led to the beginning of WiST.

Since 2017, WiST has developed a robust fellowship program for female college and graduate students to earn fully paid internships and has curated other inclusive opportunities in sports tech, including networking events, career network platforms, and seminars for middle and high school girls. Since its inception, WiST has maintained three core principles: to have a multigenerational team to leverage expertise from all backgrounds; to have support of male champions to embrace this change; and to take action for change and make a lasting impact on the sports tech industry and the lives of the people they touch. The WiST team reflects exactly what Marilou didn't see during her career in sports: a group of both women and men who are ethnically and technically diverse with different levels of experience and varied networks of connections, all who were determined to "#changetheratio" for women in the sports tech industry.[107]

Marilou garners her competitive spirit and determination for being a catalyst to enhance diversity from her experience as a lifelong athlete. When we discussed her running career at UNC, she said "I'm very lucky. I benefited directly from the early days of Title IX, enabling me to play all the sports I loved in high school. While I ran for Carolina, I was also one of the early recruits to play soccer there, receiving one of the first scholarships given to women collegiate athletes. It was very rewarding for my daughters, Kelly and Darcy, who I had coached for many years when they were young players, to receive scholarships to play soccer at Carolina for Hall of Fame coach Anson Dorrance."

Marilou founded her first company, Vivo Girl Sports, in 2009. As a mother of two elite athlete girls, she knew there was nothing in society to support them. She said, "Girls just face extraordinarily harder challenges as teenagers, especially when it comes to having support to play their sports, to the point that a vast majority actually quit playing by the age of thirteen."

In response, the Vivo Girls Sports team built a robust and rich girls and women's online sports community, providing a wealth of resources, information, and community to support girls to keep playing. Through this endeavor, Marilou realized how much she enjoyed building companies and teams. She said founding and building her start-up was like

---

107 "Home Page," Women in Sports Tech, accessed March 2, 2021.

"building the infrastructure to solve the problem from the ground up. You buy the URL, you recruit teammates smarter than you, you build the brand and the business together. You all row the boat in the same direction." Within six months they had built an interactive, vibrant website and an audience of fifty thousand girls globally. Within a year they raised one million dollars and generated $100,000 in revenue from sponsors. "I like to get s*** done," Marilou said. "I like to move fast to solve problems that make me crazy. I want to embrace innovative ideas. I don't do well bogged down in a whole bunch of bureaucracy. We eventually sold the company to Sports Endeavors in North Carolina and our team and investors were thrilled with our impact. We inspired espnW and numerous others to focus on this massive cohort of *customers* like never before."

Marilou told me, "My competitive nature and ability to inspire and empower others—those are actually my superpowers." She realized when she was in a position to build teams and be around people who shared her same competitiveness, she not only made herself and others better, but she built successful businesses with impact and purpose. As a little girl, Marilou didn't think of herself as a leader. Instead, she instilled confidence in every person she could, a skill she carried into motherhood.

> "I'm going to give you the self-belief, self-confidence, and courage to be your best and become an extraordinary leader."

MARILOU MCFARLANE

She believes that being a great leader requires you to leverage your superpowers as best you can and bring out the best in others. She said, "No one's good at everything. No leader has domain expertise at everything they're trying to do. I've always wanted to surround myself with the smartest people at what they do and then let them run with it." The best leader understands how unique superpowers from different people can join together and create a force multiplier that no one could've envisioned otherwise. She said, "Whatever leadership role you're in, it's important that you educate yourself as best you can."

Focusing in on your superpowers fulfills your passions and amplifies your talents. You may not be able to recognize Superheroes, because like Mary and Marilou, some people's superpowers are at work in subtle ways. It's important to not only figure out your superpowers but also to seek out people who possess superpowers that resonate with you.

SUPERPOWERS WORKSHOP

Up to this point, you've read about my journey of discovering my superpowers, along with the journeys of successful women infused throughout these chapters.

Now, it's your turn to explore your superpowers.

The exercise below may not be actionable for you immediately. It took me years of reflection, trial, and error to understand what my true superpowers are. I know that the complexity and breadth to which I understand how to exercise my superpowers are a lifelong journey. Write down what you believe to be your superpowers, even if you're unsure.

Before you start, remember:

- There's no such thing as having the perfect superpower.
- There's no limit to your superpowers.
- Your superpowers are what *you* know to be true about *yourself*, not what anyone else thinks.
- Your superpower can be as small or as large as you know it to be.
- Listen to your gut.

What is one of your superpowers?

_____

- How does this superpower fulfill you?

_____

- How does this superpower elevate the lives of others?

_____

When will you check on your superpowers and add to your superpowers list?

- Set a schedule or reasons for when you need to refer back to your superpowers.

CHAPTER 14

GO BE A SUPERHERO

Our team bus, wrapped in our Georgetown Hoyas logo and bulldog mascot, pulled into the Major League Soccer San Jose Earthquakes soccer stadium, where I was about to compete in the last and most important game of my career. I pulled my pre-wrap off the top of my head, letting my stray hairs go wild. I released my ponytail, struggling like I always did to untangle my curls and the rubber band at the end of my hair. I grabbed my full curly head of hair I had lightened all season with the help of John Frieda hair spray and pulled it into a tight low ponytail while keeping my focused gaze on the floor of the bus. I grabbed the white pre-wrap around my neck and carefully pulled it over my hairline, catching all of the strays to finish off my perfectly imperfect pony.

I found my Bath & Body Works Brown Sugar and Fig traveling spray bottle and sprayed my collar twice. I put my bright turquoise Beats headphones on, opened up Spotify on my phone, and typed in "Marilyn Monroe" by Nicki Minaj. Nicki always hyped me up and made me feel empowered while I focused my attention on the task at hand: winning.

Our team arose and walked confidently off the bus into the locker room, awaiting our warm-up for the NCAA College Cup Final Four, where we would face University of Southern California (USC) for a spot in the NCAA National Championship game.

As our game was about to start on the most perfectly manicured grass, the referees called the captains from both teams. I jogged to my coach, verified which side we wanted, and joined the referee and the two USC captains at the halfway line. This was the most important game of my life and the history of Georgetown Women's Soccer at the time. It was just the luck of the draw that my last game would be played in my home state of California against women I had grown up competing against.

Facing USC's two captains brought me right back to almost every weekend growing up, competing in intense tournaments against their teams. I tried to act seriously but couldn't help but laugh humbly as I stood across from two women whose careers had developed as mine had. At this pivotal point in our lives, we weren't just fighting for a National Championship, but also for our last collegiate soccer seasons. It seemed serendipitous that we would close our soccer journeys together. We had respected one another all our lives, and our competitive nature, hard work, and passion for the game had brought us back to this very spot. It's a moment I imagine C-Suite executives have when they meet their counterparts at conferences or across the table in investor meetings. We had a mutual respect for those who lived similar journeys apart, but together, nonetheless.

We ended up losing the game to USC, 0-1, as USC scored with eight minutes left in the game. For a couple of years after that loss, all I could think about was what I could've done better and what our team could've done better, often waking up with nightmares about goal scoring opportunities I missed. I was sad about it for two years; letting go of both soccer and my teammates who became my sisters was extremely hard. The entire soccer community will forever be a large part of who I am. As I have slowly overcome the hump—mostly due to time and not wanting to be stuck in the past—I can see my wonderful journey much clearer now.

In 2009, just seven years prior, I attended the NCAA College Cup National Championship game as a freshman in high school. The University of North Carolina at Chapel Hill was playing Stanford University in College Station, Texas, where we my club team also had a tournament. I remember fixating on UNC's tall, blonde outside back. She wasn't extremely fast, but she was an insanely hard worker, disrupted many of Stanford's offensive plays, and had a confident presence that stuck out.

This was the first time I felt like I saw myself in someone else. She represented the type of player I thought I could be. I was starting to grow taller and stronger. I would grow four inches my freshman year, and three more my sophomore. I was physically becoming that force that would enter college at six feet tall. Mentally, I was testing the limits of how far I could push myself.

I came home after we lost the College Cup Final Four and started rummaging through all of my sports memorabilia.

I smiled at the first club soccer practice shirts I ever wore, with old blue stains on them from the snow cone machines at the tournaments. I found the volleyball shirt I exchanged at a Junior Olympics volleyball tournament with a Puerto Rican team. Then, I found my 2009 NCAA College Cup Soccer shirt with North Carolina, Stanford, Notre Dame, and UCLA stamped on it. *"No way"* I said to myself, as my eyes started to water. Never had I imagined that I would have that same shirt with Georgetown University proudly on it or that a hopeful young girl in the stands at the 2009 tournament would play in that same game in 2016.

It took seven years. I had forgotten about my moment sitting in the stands in 2009, choosing the tall blonde outside back as my Superhero because she looked like me.

I believe our adolescent pipe dreams, mermaid scales, and superpowers always stay with us, swirling around in our veins and manifesting themselves in magical ways.

LEARNING TO JUGGLE

When I was nine, I had my first soccer tryout for the Southern California Blues, one of the top club soccer programs in the country. The first thing the coach asked me to do was juggle the soccer ball. I started to tremble because I didn't know how. To juggle a soccer ball means to suspend the ball in the air with a body part other than your hands, without letting the ball hit the ground. Juggling is a rite of passage in competitive adolescent soccer, and it's one of the first skills the club programs teach you how to master.

I couldn't pick the ball up with my feet, so my coach allowed me to pick it up with my hands. I dropped the ball on my dominant right foot, and it went flying off the field. The team looked at me with shocked eyes because all the other girls had already mastered juggling. I wanted nothing more than to leave that soccer tryout and never be seen again. I stayed in that practice, though, and when it came down to the sprints in the end, I ran as hard as I could. I didn't have the technical skills, but I was relentless in my spirits. The coach called my dad after the tryout and asked if I wanted to be a part of the team. "Are you *sure* he said that?" I asked my dad.

This tryout became one of the most important of my life, because it exposed me to a community that helped elevate me to a level I wouldn't have achieved on my own.

I've learned over the years that leadership is like learning how to juggle a soccer ball. When you first begin juggling, you're learning your footing, gaining awareness of your body position, and just trying to keep the ball in the air. The ball may go flying in all directions, and sometimes it even hits you in the face. You improve with repetitions and resilience—how willing you are to retrieve the ball you launched ten yards away, wiggle your tingling nose after the ball hits it, and start over.

Juggling was my greatest fear, but once I learned to master it, it became the thing I used to help me get in the right mindset for practice and games. Juggling taught me that there's nothing I can't learn. Once I learned how to juggle, I gained the confidence in all other aspects of my game. I knew that

I wasn't just a hard worker, but also that I relied on my work ethic to help me improve in different skills. I relentlessly studied how players performed certain moves and fearlessly tried to excel in those myself.

When you train your mind to know that you can learn anything, you stop seeing the world and opportunities as *limited* and start seeing them as *limitless*. When I stopped thinking about how to get to three hundred juggles like my teammates and started focusing on getting to my second juggle, I didn't think about the 298 other juggles that I needed to keep up. Instead, I measured what I needed to do in order to get to the next juggle. I learned how I needed to position my body and my foot, where I needed to place the ball in the air, the focus I needed to have, and how much space was around me in order to get to my next juggle. I wasn't capped at three hundred juggles; my juggles became *limitless*.

Leadership, like juggling a soccer ball, is focusing on all of the individual, subsequent juggles that help you achieve lofty results—whether that be building team culture, measuring sales performance, or inventing new products. Leadership is only defined by those results because it represents the cumulation of every little decision a leader makes—even the times when the ball hits the ground and you have to start over.

Many of the Superhero women I talked to, who have far surpassed any accolade I have ever achieved, don't necessarily set out to be a gold medalist every day of their lives. They have a dream of where they want to go, but in the minute details, they focus on doing their best and being exactly who they are. Their commitment to their process—having fun, being resilient, being good to others, being vulnerable, feeling passionate, and believing in themselves—is what molds them into the leaders they are and what keeps their Superhero capes boldly billowing. They own their details and commit wholeheartedly to their way, and as a result, they become their own unique Superhero.

As you embark on your life and leadership journey, I humbly ask that you remember and take to heart two simple-sounding but very complex things. They will be a daily practice and chore, but they will bring you the most fulfillment and joy you've ever experienced.

First, figure out who you are and love that person wholeheartedly, as much as you can. It's really f***ing hard. It's really, really f***ing hard. Put in the work to find yourself and what makes you, *you*. To be *me* means accepting that every white shirt I own has a salsa stain. I'm my goofiness and my quirks along with my competitive and driven personality wrapped into one. Never let *you* go. Own your superpowers.

Second, leave every person better than you found them. They may not look like you, think like you, or share the same humor, priorities, religion, political values, or human values as you. Still, leave them better than you found them. This includes *every* interaction, whether you're at the grocery store, in a conference room, or on social media. We each owe it to the world to treat people with kindness and respect. Spread your superpowers.

When you do these two things, you practice them daily, and you live them truly, you'll become a Superhero in your own way by bringing out the magic in yourself and every life you touch.

The superlative "Best to Walk Behind" once sexualized me, demeaned me, and locked me into a cage. However, awakening my superpowers loosened the bolts of that cage. Understanding how to use my superpowers freed me from that cage. And unleashing my superpowers now helps me inspire the magic in others. I realized "Best to Walk Behind" is my superlative, but now I choose it to mean that I'm a leader, and I'll pull everyone up behind me.

Ignite the world.

Go be a Superhero.

And don't ever stop.

ACKNOWLEDGEMENTS

To all the people who believed in me and supported me on this journey: your pep-talks and motivation propelled me to give my soul to this piece of work. Thank you for your friendship and love:

Kaitlin Brenn, Taj Johnson, William Lynch, Regina Finnegan, William Finkelstein, Dyzhanay Burton, Kelly Fitzgerald, Jordan Magnin, Classye James, Naomi Meiburger, Neveah Bradshaw, Patti White, Kimberly Sullivan, Alyssa Cronin, Wendy Grand Pre, Natalie Maciolek, Lizzy Denihan, Francine Sinatra-Anderson, Samantha Baker, Claire Magliola, Kasia Galica, Chase Wheatley, Carson Nizialek, Branden Allen, Paulette Grand Pre, Colleen D. Kroening, Allie Foard, Valli Gideons, Harper Gideons, Meghan Shaver, Max Lies, Craig Hoffman, Allie Hastings, Jenna Staudt, Claudia Pagnozzi-Schwam, David Kurtyka, Ally Manfrini, Eric Koester, Michael Karam, Michael Cannan, Sharon Kim, Lara Matetich, Ashley Nichols, Diana Necula, Cassandra Ziegler, Franziska Boelke, Julia Reshke, Rachel Sandler, Sydney Gorman, Kristin Askew, Taylor Ayres, Ali Lonner, Leah Leachman, Julianne E. Reed, Rachel Willis, Julie Beltz, Janie

Crawford, Haley Pierce, Alex Perrin, Chris Perrin, Melissa Pickrell, Maggie Meagher, Brian Celsi, Mere Chambers, Rachel Charity, Emily Welch, Amanda Sylvia, Hanna Monson, Cristina DeBiase, Chad Heal, Robert Rains, Marilou McFarlane, Craig McFarlane, Drew Topor, Ryan Houlihan, Preston Grand Pre, Faher Elfayez, Arielle Schechtman, Jo Dell Coy, Alexandra Rotatori, Adam Backels, Vikki Nguyen, Akina Newbraugh, Alexandra Shabo, Rachel Geicke, Mackenzie Hester, Fiana Gertsberg, Danielle White, Jasmine Graham, Caroline Cannan, Olivia Obermeyer, Beth Wolpman, Rick Bricker, Chris Paul, Tom Armbruster, Amber Munerlyn, Lori Ott, Jasmine Perkins, Ronald Bradford, Mara Paul, Morgan Dickson, Hollis Dana, Mikayla Harris, Hanna Monson, Amelia McNamara, Cassandra Bouton, Benedicte Engen, Christina Orcino, Bryce Blanton, Juli Marshall Cole, Kaitlin Whitehorn, Alexandra Rotatori, Mary Kroening, Maggie Nemecz, Patrick Finnegan, Leah McCullough, Graham Turner, Lyndse Hokanson, Sally Moriarty, Shriya Patnam, Chanel Stewart, Charisse M. Williams, Nikki Derbyshire, Ann Morgenstern, Juliette Medina, Kristen Vondrak, Sophie Grueterich, Avery Bush, Katyn Ott, Kelly McCann, Grace Damaska, Coleman Edmond, Moriah Dick, Amanda La Joie, and Christina Mangels.

To my interviewees: you were there for me when I asked for help, and you provided me with a lifetime of knowledge. You awoke my superpowers, made my Superheroism sizzle in my veins as I wrote, and ignited me to channel my magic into this book. My greatest hope is that my writing displays your Superheroism to those who read this book. Thank you, my Superheroes, with all my heart:

Jasmine Graham, Kristian Edwards, Valorie Kondos Field, Lydia Patterson, Maryanne Lavan, Jordyn Wieber, Mona Garcia, Haley Rosen, Dyzhanay Burton, Princess Ifon, Koma Gandy Fischbein, Yana-Janell Scott, Classye James, MJ Park, Regina Finnegan, Jesse Draper, Lyndse Hokanson, Anne Mahlum, Agatha Kluk, Rachel Geicke, Marilou McFarlane, and Jessica David.

To my two editors who became my sisters through this process: thank you for seeing me and pushing me to actualize my gut feelings. Thank you for turning disorganized chaos into organized conviction. There is no *Becoming a Superhero* without you. I love you, dearly, Amanda Munro and Jessica Fleischman.

APPENDIX

CHAPTER 1: CALLING ALL FUTURE SUPERHEROES

Stein, Leigh. "The End of the Girlboss is Here." *Gen Medium*. June 22, 2020. https://www. gen.medium.com/the-end-of-the-girl-boss-is-nigh-4591dec34ed8.

CHAPTER 2: DEFINING A SUPERHERO

Meyers, Dvora. "Valorie Kondos-Field Let Her Gymnasts Feel Her Malignant Breast Tumor." *Deadspin*. September 22, 2017. https://deadspin.com/valorie-kondos-field-let-her-gymnasts-feel-her-malignan-1818591919.

Official Miss Val. "About." Accessed January 24, 2021. https://officialmissval.com/about/.

Player's Tribune. "How Miss Val Became a Gymnastics Coaching Legend." April 25, 2019. Video, 10:52. https://www.youtube.com/watch?v=gZF6GKzBLQo.

Stolberg, Sheryl Gay and Noah Weiland. "Fauci Says U.S. Could Reach 100,000 Virus Cases a Day as Warnings Grow Darker." *New York Times*. July 13, 2020. https://www.nytimes.com/2020/06/30/us/politics/fauci-coronavirus.html.

TEDWomen 2019. "Valorie Kondos Field: Why Winning Doesn't Always Equal Success." December 2019. Video, 15:41. https://www.ted.com/talks/valorie_kondos_field_why_winning_doesn_t_always_equal_success?language=en.

UCLA. "Valorie Kondos Field '97: 2019 Professional Achievement Award." *UCLA Alumni*. April 1, 2019. https://alumni.ucla.edu/awards/valorie-kondos-field-87/#:~:text=2019%20Professional%20Achievement%20Award,Women's%20Gymnastics%20team%20defines%20optimism.

CHAPTER 3: FIRST BUT NOT LAST

After Class, Partner Empowerment by Class Pass. "Fitness Market Profile: New York City." *Fitness Industry Trends*. Accessed February 19, 2021. https://classpass.com/afterclass/fitness-market-profile-new-york-city/.

Bantz, Phillip. "More Minority, Women General Counsel at Top US Companies than Ever Before." Law.com: Corporate Counsel. August 31, 2020. https://www.law.com/corpcounsel/2020/08/31/more-minority-women-general-counsel-at-top-us-companies-than-ever-before/?slreturn=20210201235307.

Carter, Brenda Choresi. "Seeking Reflective Leadership, Voters Elect Kamala Harris." *Reflective Democracy Campaign*. November 7, 2020. https://wholeads.us/kamala-harris-vice-president/.

Center for American Women and Politics. "Women in the U.S. Congress 2021." *Eagleton Institute of Politics.* Rutgers, The State University of New Jersey. 2021. https://cawp.rutgers.edu/women-us-congress-2021.

Center for American Women and Politics. "Women of Color in Elective Office 2021." *Eagleton Institute of Politics.* Rutgers, The State University of New Jersey. 2021. https://cawp.rutgers.edu/women-color-elective-office-2021.

Deliso, Meredith. "Kamala Harris set to Make History as 1st Woman of Color to be Vice President." *The New York Times.* January 20, 2021. https://abcnews.go.com/Politics/kamala-harris-makes-history-woman-person-color-vice/story?id=73999923.

Fortune. "Fortune 500: Lockhead Martin." Fortune 500 Ranking. Updated February 2, 2021. https://fortune.com/company/lockheed-martin/fortune500/.

Harris, Kamala. "Undaunted by the Fight." Lecture. Spelman College. Atlanta, Georgia. October 26, 2018. https://www.spelman.edu/about-us/news-and-events/kamala-harris.

Harris, Rachel L. "Kamala Harris's Nomination Is Everything to Me." *The New York Times.* August 15, 2020. *https://www.nytimes.com/2020/08/15/opinion/kamala-harris-vice-president-biden.html.*

Kim, Catherine and Zack Stanton. "55 Things You Need to Know About Kamala Harris." *Politico.* August 11, 2020. https://www.

politico.com/news/magazine/2020/08/11/kamala-harris-vp-background-bio-biden-running-mate-2020-393885.

Reimann, Nicholas. "Biden Picked A 'Cop': Some on Left Slam Choice Of Kamala Harris For VP." *Forbes*. August 11, 2020. https://www.forbes.com/sites/nicholasreimann/2020/08/11/biden-picked-a-cop-some-on-left-slam-choice-of-kamala-harris-for-vp/?sh=3576e22e2b23.

U.S. Census Bureau. "Quick Facts, by Age and Sex." Table 2. Accessed January 27, 2021. https://www.census.gov/quickfacts/fact/table/US/LFE046219.

US News. "Historically Black Colleges and Universities." Best Colleges: US News & World Report Rankings. Updated 2021. https://www.usnews.com/best-colleges/rankings/hbcu.

CHAPTER 4: YOU SEEING YOU

Athnet. "Bridging the Gender Gap: The Positive Effects of Title IX." Accessed: March 1, 2021. https://www.athleticscholarships.net/title-ix-college-athletics-.3.htm#:~:text=Title%20IX%20is%20providing%20more%20opportunities%20for%20women.&text=As%20Title%20IX%20allowed%20more,percent%20of%20all%20medical%20degrees.

Businesswire. "Sports - $614 Billion Global Market Opportunities & Strategies to 2022 - ResearchAndMarkets.com." Updated May 14, 2019. https://www.businesswire.com/news/home/20190514005472/en/Sports---614-Billion-Global-Market-Opportunities-Strategies-to-2022---ResearchAndMarkets.com.

Cook, Bob. "Inside the Numbers on Girls' Participation in High School Sports." *Lifestyle* (blog). *Forbes*, March 30, 2019. https://www.forbes.com/sites/bobcook/2019/03/30/inside-the-numbers-on-girls-participation-in-high-school-sports/?sh=33c-1defc640c.

History.com. "Title IX Enacted." Accessed March 1, 2021. https://www.history.com/this-day-in-history/title-ix-enacted.

Springer, Shira. "7 Ways to Improve Coverage of Women's Sports." *Nieman Reports*, January 7, 2019. https://niemanreports.org/articles/covering-womens-sports/.

USWNT. "Kelley O'Hara." US Soccer: Kelley O'Hara. February 15, 2021. https://www.ussoccer.com/players/o/kelley-ohara.

CHAPTER 5: CHOOSE YOUR FIGHT

Beheshti, Naz. "5 Timely Leadership Lessons From 'R.B.G.': The Oscar-Nominated Documentary About Ruth Bader Ginsberg." *Forbes*. March 28, 2019. https://www.forbes.com/sites/nazbeheshti/2019/03/28/5-timely-leadership-lessons-from-r-b-g-the-oscar-nominated-documentary-about-ruth-bader-ginsberg/#5afe4bb71482.

Oyez. "Ruth Bader Ginsburg." Accessed January 28, 2021. https://www.oyez.org/justices/ruth_bader_ginsburg.

Rosen, Samantha. "How Ruth Bader Ginsburg Paved the Way for Women to Get Credit Cards." *Time*. November 13, 2020. https://time.com/nextadvisor/credit-cards/ruth-bader-ginsburg-credit-card-legacy/.

CHAPTER 6: BELIEVE YOUR WORTH

Brown, Brené. "The Power of Vulnerability." Filmed June 2010 at TEDxHouston. Houston, TX. *TED* video, 20:04. https://www.ted.com/talks/brene_brown_the_power_of_vulnerability?language=en.

Caceres, Vanessa. Eating Disorder Statistics. US News. February 14, 2020. https://health.usnews.com/conditions/eating-disorder/articles/eating-disorder-statistics.

CHAPTER 7: GET BACK UP

Anderson, Peggy. "Great Quotes from Great Women." Simple Truths. Imprint of Sourcebooks, Inc. Illinois. Book. P. 17. 2017

Back On My Feet. "Impact." Accessed March 2, 2021. https://backonmyfeet.org/program/impact/.

Cruz, Melissa. "Why Male Gymnasts Don't Do The Balance Beam." *Bustle.* August 11, 2016. https://www.bustle.com/articles/178101-why-dont-male-gymnasts-do-the-balance-beam-this-olympic-event-could-use-a-modern-update#:~:text=Male%20and%20female%20gymnasts%20compete,only%20women%20athletes%20use%20it.

Encyclopedia Britannica. "Balance beam." June 13, 2016. https://www.britannica.com/sports/balance-beam.

Fausset, Richard. "What We Know About the Shooting Death of Ahmaud Arbery." *The New York Times.* December 17, 2020. https://www.nytimes.com/article/ahmaud-arbery-shooting-georgia.html.

Merriam-Webster. s.v. "resilience (adj.)." Accessed January 21, 2021. https://www.merriam-webster.com/dictionary/resilient.

Minkoff, Rebecca. "Anne Mahlum Gets to the Core of the Matter." *Superhero Women.* Produced by Rebecca Minkoff. Podcast, 28:20. November 2019. https://anchor.fm/superwomen/support.

NBC Sports. "How the Fierce Five Olympic Gymnastics Team got its Nickname." OlympicTalk. April 16, 2020. https://olympics. nbcsports.com/2020/04/16/fierce-five-olympic-gymnastics-team-nickname/.

Wieber, Jordan. "How One Olympian Turned Devastation into Inspiration" Filmed July 16, 2019, at TEDxUCLA. Los Angeles, CA. *TEDx* video, 11:07. https://www.youtube.com/watch?v=2B_Li9wjyn4.

CHAPTER 8: BECOME THE LEADER OF YOUR OWN LIFE

Altucher, James. "What I Learned from Spanx Founder Sara Blakely." *The James Altucher Show*, Episode #211. February 7, 2017. Podcast, 1:24:02.

Blakely, Sarah. "One year ago today..." Facebook. Video, 0:53. https://www.facebook.com/watch/?v=469407126775079.

Doyle, Glennon. *Untamed.* New York: The Dial Press. 2020.

Kenyon, David. "The Best Soccer Players in United States Women's National Team History." *Bleacher Report.* June 4, 2019. https:// bleacherreport.com/articles/2838398-the-best-soccer-players-in-united-states-womens-national-team-history.

Wolny, Nick. "Spanx Founder Sara Blakely Says This Business Idea Validation Step Can Be A Big Mistake." *Entrepreneur.* November 4, 2020. https://www.entrepreneur.com/article/358381.

CHAPTER 9: BYE FEMALE RIVALRIES, HELLO FEMALE TEAMMATES

Back, Grace. "Why Do We Continue to Glorify Female Rivalry? Let's Move On." *Marie Claire.* April 8, 2019. https://www.marieclaire.com.au/female-rivalry.

Kiner, Mikaela. "It's Time to Break the Cycle of Female Rivalry." *Harvard Business Review.* April 14, 2020. https://hbr.org/2020/04/its-time-to-break-the-cycle-of-female-rivalry.

CHAPTER 10: THE SISTERHOOD EFFECT

Bernstein, Amy, Amy Galo, and Emily Caufield. "Sisterhood is Critical to Racial Justice." *Women at Work by Harvard Business Review.* Podcast. Season 5, Episode 9. 64:59. June 8, 2020.

Bernstein, Amy, Amy Galo, and Emily Caufield. "Sisterhood is Power." *Women at Work by Harvard Business Review.* Podcast. Season 2, Episode 10. 51:48:59. November 19, 2018.

Biography.com Editors. "Robin Roberts Biography." *A&E Television Networks.* April 16, 2020. https://www.biography.com/personality/robin-roberts.

ESPN.com, "About the Award: Arthur Ashe," *ESPN Internet Ventures.* Copyright 2012. http://www.espn.com/espys/arthurasheaward.

Livingston, Beth A. and Tina R. Opie. "Even at 'Inclusive' Companies, Women of Color Don't Feel Supported." *Harvard Business Review.* August 29, 2018. https://hbr.org/2019/08/even-at-inclusive-companies-women-of-color-dont-feel-supported?referral=03759&cm_vc=rr_item_page.bottom.

Mauri, Terence. "Why Sisterhood Matters on International Women's Day." *Inc..* March 8, 2018. https://www.inc.com/terence-mauri/whos-got-your-back-on-international-womens-day.html.

Minority Business Development Agency. "The Number of Firms Owned by Minority Women has Grown 163% since 2007." *U.S. Department of Commerce.* Blog. August 2018. https://www.mbda.gov/news/blog/2018/08/number-firms-owned-minority-women-has-grown-163-2007.

Piacenza, Joanna. "Sisterhood in the Workplace Only Goes So Far When It Comes to Perceptions of Pay." *Morning Consult.* May 10, 2019. https://morningconsult.com/2019/05/10/Sisterhood-in-the-workplace-only-goes-so-far-when-it-comes-to-perceptions-of-pay/.

SportsCenterJSA. "Robin Roberts' Inspiring Award Acceptance Speech." Video, 7:05. July 18, 2013. https://www.youtube.com/watch?v=1dlN3OHNxAE.

Ward, Marguerite and Rachel Premack. "What is a Microaggression? 14 Things People Think are Fine to Say at Work — but are Actually Racist, Sexist, or Offensive." *Business Insider.* July 24, 2020. https://www.businessinsider.com/microaggression-unconscious-bias-at-work-2018-6#youre-so-articulate-1.

CHAPTER 11: THE RISE AND FALL OF FEMALE LEADERS

Barret, Victoria. "Nasty Gal's Sophia Amoruso: Fashion's New Phenom." *Forbes.* June 28, 2012. https://www.forbes.com/sites/victoriabarret/2012/06/28/nasty-gals-sophia-amoruso-fashions-new-phenom/?sh=2b0c0bcb204a.

Biron, Bethany. "The 118-year Rise and Fall of JCPenney, one of America's Largest Department Stores." *Business Insider.* May 15, 2020. https://www.businessinsider.com/jcpenney-dramatic-decline-history-photos-2019-5#sales-began-to-fall-dramatically-during-the-recession-and-under-the-leadership-of-ceo-myron-ullman-by-the-end-of-2010-sales-had-dropped-by-10-from-its-2006-high-of-20-billion-10.

Bruckmüller, Susanne and Nyla R. Branscombe. "How Women End Up on the 'Glass Cliff.'" *Harvard Business Review.* January - February Edition 2011. https://hbr.org/2011/01/how-women-end-up-on-the-glass-cliff.

Cao, Sissi. "A Conversation with Sophia Amoruso, the 'Girlboss' Founder of Nasty Gal." *Observer.* October 2, 2018. https://observer.com/2018/10/sophia-amoruso-girlboss-nasty-gal/.

Coen, Buster. "11 Critical Moments from Marissa Mayer's Rocky Time as Yahoo's CEO." *The Street.* June 13, 2017. https://www.thestreet.com/investing/stocks/11-critical-moments-from-marissa-mayer-s-rocky-tenure-at-yahoo-html.

Cook, Allison and Christy Glass. "Above the Glass Ceiling: When are Women and Racial / Ethnic Minorities Promoted to CEO?" *Wiley Online Library.* Published June 10, 2013. https://onlinelibrary.wiley.com/doi/full/10.1002/smj.2161.

Dishman, Lydia. "It's the End of an Era for #Girlboss as Founder and CEO Sophia Amoruso Steps Down," *Fast Company*, June 22, 2020. https://www.fastcompany.com/90519787/its-the-end-of-an-era-for-girlboss-as-founder-and-ceo-sophia-amoruso-steps-down#:~:text=Sophia%20Amoruso%2C%20the%20outspoken%20founder,move%20in%20an%20Instagram%20post.&text=Until%20now%3A%20Amoruso%20says%20she's,leaving%20along%20with%2010%20others.

Dishman, Lydia. "What is the Glass Cliff, and Why Do So Many Female CEOs Fall Off It?" *Fast Company*. July 27, 2018. https://www.fastcompany.com/90206067/what-is-the-glass-cliff-and-why-do-so-many-female-ceos-fall-off-it.

Hoffower, Hillary. "The Fall of the Girlboss is Acutally a Good Thing." *Business Insider*. July 26, 2020. https://www.businessinsider.com/rise-and-fall-girl-boss-analysis-2020-7.

Mull, Amanda. "The Girlboss Has Left the Building." *The Atlantic*. June 25, 2020. https://www.theatlantic.com/health/archive/2020/06/girlbosses-what-comes-next/613519/.

O'Connor, Clare. "As Nasty Gal Files Bankruptcy, Founder Sophia Amoruso's Fortune Decimated." *Forbes*. November 11, 2016. https://www.forbes.com/sites/clareoconnor/2016/11/11/as-nasty-gal-files-bankruptcy-founder-sophia-amorusos-fortune-decimated/?sh=a46f89d6da88.

Perlroth, Nicole. "Naughty in Name Only." *The New York Times*. March 24, 2013. https://www.nytimes.com/2013/03/25/technology/nasty-gal-an-online-start-up-is-a-fast-growing-retailer.html.

Stein, Leigh. "The End of the Girlboss is Here." *Medium: Gen.* June 22, 2020. https://gen.medium.com/the-end-of-the-girlboss-is-nigh-4591dec34ed8.

Stewart, Emily. "Why Struggling Companies Promote Women: The Glass Cliff, Explained." *Vox.* October 31, 2018. https://www.vox.com/2018/10/31/17960156/what-is-the-glass-cliff-women-ceos.

CHAPTER 12: INVEST IN HUMAN CAPITAL

Draper, Jesse. "Investing in Women Isn't a Fucking Charity," *Medium*, September 28, 2020. https://medium.com/@jessecdraper/investing-in-women-isnt-a-fucking-charity-ceabe8918b9c.

The Harvard Gazette, "Koma Gandy Fischbein '95 Elected Chief Marshal," *The Harvard Gazette*, February 13, 2020. https://news.harvard.edu/gazette/story/2020/02/koma-gandy-fischbein-to-serve-as-chief-marshal-at-369th-commencement/.

CHAPTER 13: DEFINE YOUR SUPERPOWERS

Kenton, Will. "What is the Big 4." *Investopedia.* January 7, 2021. https://www.investopedia.com/terms/b/bigfour.asp.

US News. "2021 Best Business Schools." *US News.* 2020. https://www.usnews.com/best-graduate-schools/top-business-schools/mba-rankings.

Women's Bond Club. "Rising Star Award." Accessed March 2, 2021. https://womensbondclub.com/WBC/Membership/Rising_Star_Award/WBC/OurPrograms/RisingStarAward.aspx-?hkey=02fd5a51-476f-405a-bf6a-8d6bdcc5073a

Women in Sports Tech. "Home Page." Accessed March 2, 2021. https://www.womeninsportstech.org/about.